TOP 10
SAN DIEGO

PAMELA BARRUS

DK

EYEWITNESS TRAVEL

Left **Hotel del Coronado** Center **Cruiseship liner at San Diego Harbor** Right **Zoo Safari Park**

LONDON, NEW YORK,
MELBOURNE, MUNICH AND DELHI
www.dk.com

Printed and bound in China

First American Edition, 2005
15 16 10 9 8 7 6

Published in the United States by DK Publishing,
345 Hudson Street, New York, New York 10014

**Reprinted with revisions 2007, 2009,
2011, 2013**
**Copyright 2005, 2013 © Dorling
Kindersley Limited, London
A Penguin company**

A catalog record for this book is available from the
Library of Congress.

ISSN 1479-344X
ISBN 978-0-75669-676-4

Within each Top 10 list in this book, no hierarchy of
quality or popularity is implied. All 10 are, in the
editor's opinion, of roughly equal merit.

MIX
Paper from
responsible sources
FSC™ C018179
www.fsc.org

Contents

San Diego's Top 10

The information in this DK Eyewitness Top 10 Travel Guide is checked regularly.
Every effort has been made to ensure that this book is as up-to-date as possible at the time of
going to press. Some details, however, such as telephone numbers, opening hours, prices,
gallery hanging arrangements and travel information are liable to change. The publishers
cannot accept responsibility for any consequences arising from the use of this book, nor for
any material on third party websites, and cannot guarantee that any website address in this
book will be a suitable source of travel information. We value the views and suggestions of
our readers very highly. Please write to: Publisher, DK Eyewitness Travel Guides,
Dorling Kindersley, 80 Strand, London, WC2R 0RL, UK, or email: travelguides@dk.com.

Cover: Front – **Corbis:** Robert Harding World Imagery/Ruth Tomlinson main; **DK Images:** Max Alexander bl.
Spine – **DK Images:** Max Alexander b. Back – **DK Images:** Chris Stowers tc, tl, tr

Left **La Jolla** Center **Souvenirs at Tijuana** Right **The Cheese Shop, Gaslamp Quarter**

Left **California Tower, Balboa Park** Right **Catedral de Nuestra Señora de Guadalupe, Tijuana**

Key to abbreviations
Adm *admission charge* **Dis. access** *disabled access*

SAN DIEGO'S
TOP 10

SAN DIEGO'S TOP 10

🔟 San Diego Highlights

Blessed by a sunny climate that never varies ten degrees from moderate and a splendid setting along the Pacific Ocean, San Diegans can well boast they live the California Dream. Although non-stop outdoor recreation, a vibrant downtown, and world-class attractions keep the city's spirit young, its heart lies in its Spanish beginnings as the birthplace of California.

Gaslamp Quarter
Old-fashioned wrought-iron gas lamps lead the way to the hottest scene in town. Rocking nightspots and a dazzling selection of restaurants give life to San Diego's original Victorian downtown *(see pp8–9).*

Embarcadero
With its nautical museums, vintage ships, and superb views across a harbor busy with sailboats, ferries, and battleships, the Embarcadero links the city to its ocean heritage *(see pp10–13).*

Balboa Park & San Diego Zoo
San Diegans take pride in having one of the finest urban parks in the world. Its famous zoo, fascinating museums, and exquisite gardens offer endless activities *(see pp14–19).*

Old Town State Historic Park
The original location and social center of San Diego until 1872, adobe houses, old wood-frame buildings, and artifacts belonging to its pioneer families have been faithfully restored *(see pp22–3).*

Coronado
This idyllic community is recognizable throughout the world by the fabulous Hotel del Coronado. Coronado's white sandy beaches, sidewalk cafés, and oceanfront mansions have enticed visitors for over a century *(see pp24–5).*

Map labels: La Jolla Bay · La Jolla **9** · TORREY PINES RD · ARDATH RD · 52 · LA JOLLA BOULEVARD · N TORREY PINES RD · GENESEE AVE · The Muirlands · Pacific Beach · GRAND AVENUE · MISSION BOULEVARD · INGRAHAM STREET · Mission Bay · Mission Beach · Mission Bay Park **8** · San Diego River · San Diego River · Ocean Beach · Loma Portal · 8 · NIMITZ BLVD · ROSECRANS ST · CANON STREET · CABRILLO MEMORIAL DR · Point Loma **6**

Previous pages: **Façade of La Casa del Padre Serra**

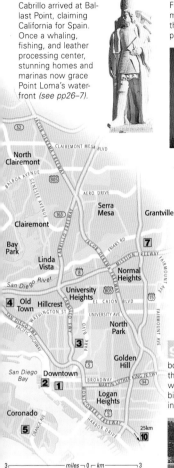

Point Loma
In 1542, Juan Cabrillo arrived at Ballast Point, claiming California for Spain. Once a whaling, fishing, and leather processing center, stunning homes and marinas now grace Point Loma's waterfront *(see pp26–7)*.

Mission Basilica San Diego de Alcalá
Father Junípero Serra established this mission in 1769. Its aim was to Christianize the Native Americans and affirm Spain's presence in California *(see pp28–9)*.

SeaWorld
At one of the premier attractions of Southern California, leaping killer whales, cavorting dolphins, and promenading sea lion divas entertain over four million visitors a year *(see pp30–31)*.

La Jolla
Multi-million-dollar seaside villas, boutiques, and elegant restaurants line the streets of this exclusive community, which is also noted for its prestigious biotech and oceanographic research institute *(see pp32–3)*.

Tijuana
Only 20 minutes south of San Diego but a whole world away, this famous border town offers great shopping and top-rated restaurants. And yes, striped burros and black velvet Elvis paintings still exist *(see pp34–5)*.

7

TOP 10 Gaslamp Quarter

A hip nightlife, trendy restaurants, and unique boutiques compete for attention in San Diego's most vibrant neighborhood. Alonzo Horton's 1867 New Town (see p38) seemed doomed to the wrecking ball in the 1970s, but a civic revitalization program transformed the dilapidated area into a showcase destination. By 1980, the Gaslamp Quarter was decreed a National Historic District with its quaint Victorian, Italianate, and Renaissance structures.

Sign for the William Heath Davis House

Gaslamp Quarter street

🧀 Stop at the Cheese Shop (627 4th Ave) for sandwiches, or at the Ghirardelli Chocolate Shop (643 5th Ave) for a hot fudge sundae.

🚗 Parking is difficult at weekends, especially if there's a ballgame over at Petco Park. Take the San Diego Trolley; it stops right at Gaslamp.

- Map J5
- www.gaslamp.org
- William Heath Davis House: 410 Island Ave (619) 233-4692; www.gaslampquarter.org; Open 10am–5pm Tue–Sat, noon–4pm Sun; Adm $5; Historical walking tours 11am Sat, $15
- Louis Bank of Commerce: 835 5th Ave
- San Diego Hardware: 840 5th Ave
- Old City Hall: 433 G St
- Balboa Theatre: 4th Ave & E St
- Yuma Building: 631 5th Ave
- Keating Building: 432 F St
- Ingle Building: 424 F St
- Lincoln Hotel: 536 5th Ave

Top 10 Features

1. William Heath Davis House
2. Louis Bank of Commerce
3. San Diego Hardware
4. Old City Hall
5. Balboa Theatre
6. Yuma Building
7. Keating Building
8. Ingle Building
9. Lincoln Hotel
10. Wrought-iron Gas Lamps

1 William Heath Davis House

Named after the man who tried but failed to develop San Diego in 1850, the museum is home to the Gaslamp Quarter Historical Foundation. It is the oldest wooden structure in downtown San Diego *(above)*.

2 Louis Bank of Commerce

A bank until 1893, this Victorian structure *(right)* became Wyatt Earp's *(see p39)* favorite bar. It once contained the Golden Poppy Hotel, a notorious brothel. Present-day offices are much tamer.

3 San Diego Hardware

Once a dance hall, then a five-and-dime store, this building housed one of San Diego's oldest businesses, founded in 1892. Though the store relocated in 2006, the original storefront remains.

4 Old City Hall

Dating from 1874, this Italianate building features 16-ft (5-m) ceilings, brick arches, Classical columns, and a wrought-iron cage elevator. In 1900, the entire city government would fit inside. Today, the building houses shops and a restaurant.

⑤ Balboa Theatre
This landmark 1,500-seat theater *(right)* started out as a grand cinema with waterfalls flanking the stage. Notice the beautiful tiled dome on the roof. A restoration project converted the building into a venue for live performances.

⑥ Yuma Building
Captain Wilcox of the US *Invincible* owned downtown's first brick structure in 1888. The building *(below)* was named for his business dealings in Yuma, Arizona. Residential lofts with bay windows now occupy its upper levels.

⑦ Keating Building
Fannie Keating built this Romanesque-style building *(above)* in 1890 in honor of her husband George. It once housed the town's most prestigious offices.

⑧ Ingle Building
The Hard Rock Café was once known as the Golden Lion Tavern. Note the lion sculptures, the stained-glass windows, and the 1906 stained-glass dome over the bar.

⑨ Lincoln Hotel
Built in 1913, the four-story tiled structure features Chinese elements, the original beveled glass in its upper stories, and its original green-and-white ceramic tile facade. Japanese prisoners were housed here before departing for internment camps during World War II.

⑩ Wrought-iron Gas Lamps
Although San Diego's historic district is named after the quaint green wrought-iron gas lamps that line the streets, they run on electricity.

Stingaree District
After its legitimate businesses relocated in the late 19th century, New Town was home to 120 brothels, opium dens, 71 saloons, and gambling halls, some operated by famous lawman Wyatt Earp. It became known as "Stingaree" because one could be stung on its streets as easily as by the stingaree fish in the bay. After police unsuccessfully tried cleaning up Stingaree in 1912, it slowly disintegrated into a slum until rescued by the Gaslamp Quarter Foundation some 50 years later.

If you want to enjoy the architecture, come during the day when the district is less crowded.

Embarcadero

Ever since Juan Cabrillo sailed into San Diego Bay in 1542 (see p38), much of the city's life has revolved around its waterfront. Pioneers stepped ashore on its banks; immigrants worked as whalers and fishermen; the US Navy left an indelible mark with its shipyards and warships. Tourism has added another layer to the harbor's lively atmosphere. The Embarcadero welcomes visitors with its art displays, walkways, nautical museums, harbor cruises, and benches on which to sit and enjoy the uninterrupted harbor activity.

Embarcadero Marina Park

🍴 For a quick bite, try Anthony's Fishette at 1360 North Harbor Drive. Sandwiches and salads are the best outdoor options.

🚲 Pedicabs are usually available to take you down to Seaport Village.

• Map G3
• Harbor Cruises: 1050 N. Harbor Dr; Narrated tours: 1 hour $20; 2 hours $25; several departures daily
• Santa Fe Depot: 1050 Kettner Blvd
• USS Midway Museum: 910 N. Harbor Dr; (619) 544-9600; Open 10am–5pm; Adm adult/child $18/$9

Top 10 Attractions

1. San Diego County Administration Center
2. San Diego Harbor
3. Maritime Museum of San Diego
4. Piers
5. Santa Fe Depot
6. USS Midway Museum
7. Tuna Harbor
8. Seaport Village
9. Embarcadero Marina Park
10. San Diego Convention Center

San Diego County Administration Center
Dedicated by President F. Roosevelt, the 1936 civic structure *(above)* looks especially magisterial when floodlit at night. Enter through the west door and feel free to wander about *(see p44)*.

San Diego Harbor
One of the greatest attractions of the Embarcadero is watching the bustling harbor, as Navy destroyers, aircraft carriers, ferries, cruise ships, and sailboats glide past. Be a part of the action by taking a harbor cruise.

Maritime Museum of San Diego
Nautical lovers can marvel at *Medea*, *Star of India (below)*, and *Berkeley*. These vintage ships have been restored to their former glory *(see p42)*.

Piers
Glistening cruise ships bound for Mexico and the Panama Canal tie up at B Street Pier. Harbor cruises and ferries to Coronado can be caught nearby.

Morning is the least crowded time to visit the Embarcadero.

Santa Fe Depot

The train cars may be modern, but the atmosphere recalls the stylish days of rail travel. The interiors of the Spanish-Colonial style building are resplendent with burnished oak benches, original tiles *(left)*, bronze-and-glass chandeliers, and wonderful friezes depicting Native American themes.

Embarcadero Marina Park

Relax on one of the grassy expanses to enjoy the excellent views of the harbor and Coronado Bridge. Joggers and bicyclists use the paths around the park *(see p47)*, and on weekends, entertainers and artists demonstrate their work.

San Diego Convention Center

The center was designed along nautical lines to complement the water-front location, with its flying buttresses, skylight tubes, and rooftop sails.

USS Midway Museum

The 1,000-ft (305-m) USS *Midway* *(see pp12–13)*, commissioned in 1945, was once the world's largest warship. Many docents on board are veterans who served on the carrier.

Seaport Village

New England and Spanish design blend eclectically in this waterfront area with brilliant harbor views *(above & p49)*.

Tuna Harbor

San Diego was once home to the world's largest tuna fleet, with 200 commercial boats. Portuguese immigrants dominated the trade until the canneries moved to Mexico and Samoa. Even today, some tuna boats remain and the US Tuna Foundation still keeps its offices here *(right)*.

San Diego & the Military

San Diego has had strong military ties ever since the Spanish built the presidio (fortress) in 1769. Hosting the largest military complex in the world, the military contributes handsomely to the local economy. Their presence is everywhere: Navy SEALS train at Coronado, three aircraft carriers and warships berth in the harbor, and Marines land amphibious tanks along Camp Pendleton. Ship parades and tours are popular events during San Diego's September/October Fleet Week.

USS *Midway*

USS Midway Museum

Hangar Deck
The hangar deck stored the carrier's aircraft, with large elevators raising planes up to the flight deck as needed. Now the carrier's entry level, it has audio-tour headsets, aircraft displays, a gift shop, café, and restrooms. Don't miss the 24-ft (7-m) Plexi-glas model of the *Midway* used by shipbuilders in World War II to construct the carrier.

Island
Sometimes called the Super-structure, ladders take you up to the navigation room and bridge, from where the ship's movements were commanded. The flight control deck oversaw aircraft operations.

Flight Deck
The area of the *Midway*'s flight deck is roughly 4 acres (1.6 ha) in size. Additional aircraft are on display here, as well as the entry to the Island. The flight deck was where dramatic take-offs and landings took place – take-offs were from the bow

Flight deck talk on the USS *Midway*

while the angled deck was used for landings.

Aircraft
More than two dozen planes and helicopters are on display on the flight and hangar decks. Among the displays are the F-14 Tomcat, which flies at speeds exceeding Mach 2, a F-4 Phantom, and A-6 Intruder. The *Midway* once held up to 80 aircraft of various types.

Galley
The *Midway* could store up to 1.5-million lbs (680,388 kg) of dry provisions and a quarter-million lbs (113,398 kg) of meat and vegetables to feed a crew who ate 13,000 meals daily.

Post Office
The *Midway*'s crew often had to wait several weeks at a time for a Carrier Onboard Delivery flight to receive letters from home. The post office was also in charge of the disbursement of money orders.

Berths
Sleeping berths for 400 of the 4,500 crew members are displayed on the hangar deck. Beds were too short to be comfortable for anyone over 6 ft (1.8 m), and the accompanying metal lockers could hold barely more than a uniform. Enlisted men were often just out of high school.

Sign up for DK's email newsletter on traveldk.com

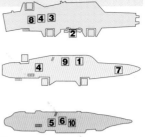

Arresting Wire & Catapults

Notice the arresting wire on the flight deck. This enabled a pilot to land a 20-ton jet cruising at 150 miles (241 km) an hour on an area the size of a tennis court. A hook attached to the tail of a plane grabbed the wire during landing. Two steam catapults helped propel the plane for take-off.

Virtual Reality Flight Simulations

For an additional price, which also includes a briefing, a flight suit, and 30 minutes of flight, you can experience flying a plane by taking the controls of a flight simulator. Also on hand are several standard flight stations, where, for another ticket, you can practice taking off from a carrier.

Key

▬ Roof Flight Deck and Island

▬ Hangar Deck and Forecastle

▬ Ground Floor 2nd, 3rd, and 4th Decks

Metal Shop

Located on the mess deck, the metal shop produced metal structures and replicated metal parts for the ship or its aircraft. Self-sufficiency and versatility were the keywords for tours of duty when the ship would be away for months at a time.

Top 10 Midway Statistics

1. Overall length: 1,001 ft, 6 inches (305 m)
2. Width: 258 ft (78.6 m)
3. Height: 222 ft, 3 inches (67.7 m)
4. Full Displacement: 70,000 tons (63,502,932 kg)
5. Number of propellers: 4
6. Weight of each propeller: 22 tons (19,958 kg)
7. Boilers: 12
8. Miles of piping: 200 (322 km)
9. Miles of copper conductor: 3,000 (4,828 km)
10. Ship fuel capacity: 2.23 million gallons (8,441,468 liters)

History of the *Midway*

Commissioned on September 10, 1945, the Midway was named after the Battle of Midway, which was the turning point for the Allies in the War of the Pacific. She remained the largest ship in the world for ten years, and was the first ship too large to transit the Panama Canal. After the fall of Saigon on April 30, 1975, she saw further action during Operation Desert Storm in 1991, and finished her years of service by evacuating military personnel threatened by the 1991 eruption of Mount Pinatubo in the Philippines. The Midway was decommissioned in 1992.

Launching of the USS *Midway*, 1945

Butterfly

⏱10 Balboa Park

Since the early 20th century, Balboa Park has awed San Diegans with its romantic hillside setting, lush landscaping, and splendid architecture. The park's magnificent Spanish architecture dates from the 1915–16 Panama-California Exposition. On weekends, thousands of visitors come to indulge their interests, whether it's for recreation, Shakespeare, or art. However, the park is probably best known as the home of the world-famous San Diego Zoo, where almost 4,000 animals and 800 species reside.

Spreckels Organ Pavilion

🍴 **Get lunch at the Japanese Sculpture Garden's Tea Pavilion.**

⏲ **Some parking lots aren't open until 8:30am.**

• Map L2
• www.balboapark.org
• House of Hospitality: (619) 239-0512; Open 9am–4:30pm daily
• San Diego Zoo: (619) 231-1515; Open 9am–5pm Sep 5–Jun 23; 9am–9pm Jun 24–Sep 4; Adm adult/child $42/$32; www.sandiegozoo.org
• Spreckels Organ Pavilion: (619) 702-8138; Concerts: 2–3pm Sun; 7:30–9pm Mon mid-Jun–Aug
• House of Pacific Relations: (619) 234-0739; Open noon–4pm Sun; www.sdhpr.org

Top 10 Attractions

1 Reuben H. Fleet Science Center
2 Casa del Prado
3 The Old Globe
4 El Cid Statue
5 California Tower and Dome
6 House of Hospitality
7 Spanish Village Art Center
8 San Diego Zoo
9 Spreckels Organ Pavilion
10 House of Pacific Relations

1 Reuben H. Fleet Science Center

Learn about electricity, digital recording, tornados, and explore sense and touch in the Gallery of Illusions and Perceptions. Catch an IMAX movie or learn some astronomy at a planetarium show *(see p52)*.

2 Casa del Prado

This outstanding structure (above) is an historical reconstruction of a building from the 1915 Panama-California Exposition. Wall reliefs commemorate Father Junípero Serra and Juan Cabrillo. It is now used for community events.

3 The Old Globe

The Tony-winning Old Globe Theatre *(below)*, Sheryl and Harvey White Theatre, and Lowell Davies Festival Theatre form a cultural resource *(see p50)*.

4 El Cid Statue

Rodrigo Diaz de Vivar, Campeador, better known as the Spanish hero El Cid, overlooks the Plaza de Panama. This 23-ft (7-m) tall bronze sculpture *(right)* was dedicated in 1930 as a symbolic guardian of Balboa Park.

6 House of Hospitality

Modeled on a hospital in Spain, this building was erected in 1915 for the Panama-California Exposition and reconstructed in the 1990s. It is now a visitors center with helpful staff.

7 Spanish Village Art Center

Richard Requa *(see p39)*, architect of the 1935–36 Exposition, wanted visitors to experience the simple life of a Spanish village. This complex now houses 37 studios where craftspeople and artists display their creations *(below & p43)*.

8 San Diego Zoo

In this zoo *(see pp16–17)*, thousands of animals thrive in re-created natural habitats. Thanks to successful breeding programs and webcams, endangered baby pandas *(below)* are now animal superstars.

5 California Tower and Dome

Built for the 1915–16 Exposition, this building *(above)* with its 200-ft (61-m) tower has come to represent San Diego's identity. Famous figures of the city's past are represented on the exquisite façade. Inside is the Museum of Man *(see p18)*.

9 Spreckels Organ Pavilion

One of the largest outdoor organs in the world contains 4,530 pipes *(below)*. The metal curtain protecting the organ weighs close to 12 tons. Free organ recitals are held every Sunday.

10 House of Pacific Relations

Founded in 1935, these cottages feature cultural ambassadors from 32 countries, who showcase their local traditions and histories.

Balboa Park & World War II

More than 2,000 beds were lined up in Balboa Park's museums to accommodate those wounded in the 1941 Pearl Harbor attack. All buildings were requisitioned for barracks. The park became one of the largest hospital training centers in the world: 600 Navy nurses were stationed at the House of Hospitality, the Old Globe Theatre became a scullery, and the lily pond served as a rehab pool. In 1947, the military returned the park to the city.

Performers at the House of Pacific Relations present ethnic songs and dances every Sunday from March to October.

15

Left **Animal show** Right **Gorilla Tropics**

San Diego Zoo

Giant Panda Research Station

The giant panda superstars spend most of their day eating bamboo, oblivious to millions of adoring fans that line up for a glimpse or to watch them via a 24-hour panda cam. Five panda births have occurred at the zoo in the last nine years, most recently male Yun Zi in August 2009. He can be seen along with his mother Bai Yum and father Gao Gao. The San Diego Zoo has the largest population of endangered giant pandas in the United States.

Polar Bear Plunge

In this recreated Arctic tundra habitat, polar bears lounge about and frolic in the chilly water of a 130,000-gallon plunge pool. Sometimes, for a special enrichment treat, zookeepers fill the enclosure with 18 tons of shaved snow for the bears to play in. Don't

Giant Panda Research Station

miss the pool viewing area down below; the bears often swim right up to the window.

Scripps Aviary

Inside a massive mesh cage, experience an exotic rainforest with sounds of cascading water and more than 130 chirping, cawing, and screeching African birds. Sit on a bench amid lush vegetation and try to spot a silvery-checked hornbill or gold-breasted starling.

Gorilla Tropics

These Western lowland gorillas romp and climb over wide areas of jungle and grassland. Parent gorillas lovingly tend to their children, while others sit quietly with chins in hand, contemplating the strange creatures on the other side of the glass.

Tiger River

A misty, orchid-filled rainforest is home to the endangered Indo-Chinese tiger. Marvel at these wondrous animals as they sit majestically on the rocks, waterfalls flowing

Polar Bear Plunge

16

For the best sightings, keep in mind that the animals feed and are more active in the mornings and late evenings.

behind them. This natural habitat was created to resemble their native jungle environment, with steep slopes, logs to climb on, and a warm cave near the viewing window.

Tarantula

Ituri Forest
Meet Otis, several thousand pounds of male hippo, who lives in this re-creation of the Congo River Basin with female Funani. The hippos share their jungle home with forest buffaloes, swamp monkeys, and okapis, whose prehensile, long black tongues enable them to grab nearby leaves to eat.

Elephant Odyssey
The endangered African and Asian elephants consume up to 125 lbs (57 kgs) of hay and 30 gallons of water a day. Keep your camera ready, as the elephants often toss barrels or scratch their back under a special roller. Asian elephants have dome-shaped backs, while the ears of an African elephant are shaped like the African continent.

Koalas
With names like Koorine and Gidgee, who can resist these cuddly guys? With the largest koala colony outside Australia, the zoo's successful breeding program enables loans to zoos worldwide, and makes financial contributions to habitat conservation programs in Australia.

Reptile House
If it slithers, hisses, or rattles, it's here. Be glad these animals, especially the king cobra, Albino python, and Gila monsters, are behind glass. Cages marked with a red dot indicate the venomous ones.

Children's Zoo

Children's Zoo
Little ones love petting the goats and sheep in the paddock (wash-up sinks are nearby), while older kids squeal with mischievous glee at the tarantulas, black-widow spiders, and hissing cockroaches. The nursery takes care of baby animals whose mothers can't look after them.

Take the double-deck bus tour first (drivers are fun and informative), and then return to what interests you.

Left **Museum of Art** Center **Museum of Man** Right **Air & Space Museum**

Balboa Park Museums

San Diego Museum of Art
This exceptional collection includes works by old masters and major 19th- and 20th-century artists. Be sure to check out its Asian art collection. ⊗ *Map L1* • *(619) 232-7931* • *Open 10am–5pm Mon, Tue, Thu–Sat (to 7pm Fri); noon–5pm Sun* • *Adm* • *www.sdmart.org*

San Diego Museum of Man
Learn about evolution from a replica of a 4-million-year-old human ancestor, and visit the mummy room. Artifacts from the Kumeyaay, San Diego's original inhabitants, and a replica of a huge Mayan monument emphasize the culture of the Americas. ⊗ *Map L1* • *(619) 239-2001* • *Open 10am–4:30pm daily* • *Adm* • *www.museumofman.org*

San Diego Natural History Museum
Galleries showcase the evolution and diversity of California. Exhibits, guided weekend nature walks, and field trips explore the natural world. ⊗ *Map M1* • *(619) 232-3821* • *Open 10am–5pm Sun–Fri, 9am–5pm Sat* • *Adm* • *www.sdnhm.org*

Timken Museum of Art
The collection includes Rembrandt's *Saint Bartholomew*, and works by Rubens and Bruegel the Elder.
⊗ *Map L1* • *(619) 239-5548* • *Open 10am–4:30pm Tue–Sat; 1:30–4:30pm Sun* • *www.timkenmuseum.org*

A portrait by Frans Hals at the Timken Museum

Mingei International Museum
The Japanese word *mingei* means "art of the people" and on view here is a display of international folk art. Exhibits include textiles, jewelry, furniture, and pottery.
⊗ *Map L1* • *(619) 239-0003* • *Open 10am–4pm Tue–Sun* • *Adm* • *www.mingei.org*

Museum of Photographic Arts
Temporary exhibitions featuring the world's most celebrated camera geniuses mix with pieces from the museum's permanent collection. The theater screens film classics.
⊗ *Map L1* • *(619) 238-7559* • *Open 10am–5pm Tue–Sun (to 9pm Thu in summer)* • *Adm* • *www.mopa.org*

San Diego History Center
An alternating collection of old photographs and artifacts that introduce San Diego's early years.
⊗ *Map L1* • *(619) 232-6203* • *Open 10am–5pm daily* • *Adm* • *www.sandiego history.org*

The **Passport to Balboa Park** *includes admission to 14 museums, the Japanese Garden, and the zoo; available at the Visitors Center.*

8 San Diego Automotive Museum

Discover California's car culture through classic vehicles, rotating themed exhibits, and educational permanent ones. A Racing Hall of Fame honors past giants of the racing world. ◎ Map L2 • (619) 231-2886 • Open 10am–5pm daily • Adm • www.sdautomuseum.org

Automotive Museum

9 San Diego Air & Space Museum

One of the museum's finest planes, the Lockheed A-12 Blackbird spy plane, greets you on arrival. Don't miss the International Aerospace Hall of Fame. ◎ Map L2 • (619) 234-8291 • Open 10am–5pm daily • Adm • www.sandiegoairandspace.org

10 San Diego Hall of Champions Sports Museum

The artifacts of San Diego's sports heroes are exhibited here. Inspiring displays cover some 40 sports. ◎ Map L2 • (619) 234-2544 • Open 10am–4:30pm daily • Adm • www.sdhoc.com

Top 10 Gardens of Balboa Park

1. Alcázar Gardens
2. Japanese Friendship Garden
3. Botanical Building & Lily Ponds
4. Palm Canyon
5. Casa del Rey Moro
6. Zoro Garden
7. Rose Garden
8. Desert Garden
9. Florida Canyon
10. Moreton Bay Fig Tree

The Mother of Balboa Park

Horticulturalist Kate Sessions needed room to establish a nursery in 1892. She struck a deal with the city of San Diego in which she promised to plant 100 trees a year in the then-called City Park and 300 trees elsewhere in exchange for 36 acres. A 35-year planting frenzy resulted in 10,000 glorious trees and shrubs, shady arbors draped with bougainvillea, and flower gardens that burst with color throughout the year.

Bougainvillea

Alcázar Gardens, inspired by the Alcázar Palace in Seville, Spain

Free trams help you get around Balboa Park and stop at designated areas.

🔟 Old Town State Historic Park

After Mexico won its independence from Spain in 1821, many retired soldiers created what is now Old Town, laying their homes and businesses around the plaza in typical Spanish style. Through trade with Boston, the town began to prosper. After a fire in 1872 destroyed much of the commercial center, San Diego moved to a "New Town" closer to the bay. Today, you can explore the preserved and restored structures of San Diego's pioneer families.

Canon in Old Town Plaza

Plaza at Old Town

🍴 Head to one of San Diego's most famous Mexican restaurants, Old Town Mexican Café & Cantina *(see p83)*, and watch the ladies make tortillas as you have lunch.

🚶 One-hour walking tours led by park staff leave daily at 11am and 2pm from the Robinson-Rose House.

Many of the park concessionaires sell a lot of kitsch; you'll do better outside the park, or try the lovely shops at Bazaar del Mundo.

• Map N5
• www.parks.ca.gov
• 4002 Wallace St
• (619) 220-5422
• Open May–Sep 10am–5pm, Oct–Apr 10am–4pm
• La Casa de Estudillo: closed Mon
• Seeley Stable Museum: closed Tue

Top 10 Sights

1. Plaza
2. La Casa de Estudillo
3. La Casa de Bandini
4. Seeley Stable Museum
5. San Diego Union Historical Museum
6. Mason Street School
7. Colorado House
8. La Casa de Machado y Stewart
9. Robinson-Rose House
10. Bazaar del Mundo

Plaza
Spanish communities used the town plaza for bullfights, political events, executions, and fiestas. Ever since the American flag was raised in 1846, tradition maintains that the Old Town flagpole must be made from a ship's mast.

La Casa de Estudillo
Built by José Estudillo, the Presidio's commander, this 1827 adobe home *(below)* is Old Town's showpiece. Workmen shaped the curved red tiles of the roof by spreading clay over their legs. Thick walls helped support the roof.

Buildings in the park

La Casa de Bandini
Peruvian Juan Bandini arrived in San Diego in 1819 and became one of its wealthiest citizens. Following business losses, his home was turned into a hotel, which still operates as the Cosmopolitan Hotel.

Seeley Stable Museum
Until railroads proved more efficient, Albert Seeley ran a stage-coach business between San Diego and LA. Today, this barn houses original carriages and wagons from the Wild West.

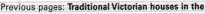

Previous pages: **Traditional Victorian houses in the Heritage Park**

San Diego Union Historical Museum
This wood-frame house *(above)* was built in New England and shipped down in 1851. Home to the early years of *The San Diego Union*, a faithful restoration depicts the newsroom of the city's oldest newspaper.

Robinson-Rose House
Docents are on hand to answer questions at this house which dates from 1853 and is the headquarters of Old Town *(below)*. Look out for the model of the 1872 Old Town.

BUILT
1853
ROBINSON·ROSE
HOUSE

Bazaar del Mundo
Vibrant colors and unique shops present the best of Latin America. Andean bands and folk dancers perform amidst Guatemalan weavings and Mexican folk art *(see p82)*.

Mason Street School
This one-room school opened in 1865. Its first teacher, Mary Chase Walker, resigned her $65-a-month position when townspeople complained that she had invited a black woman to lunch.

La Casa de Machado y Stewart
Jack Stewart married Rosa Machado in 1845 and moved to this adobe home, where the family line continued until 1966. The structure's deterioration finally compelled them to move.

Colorado House
The name Wells Fargo came to symbolize the opening of the American West. At this little museum housed in a former hotel, a restored stagecoach *(right)* is the main exhibit.

First Impressions
In his epic story of early San Diego, *Two Years Before the Mast*, published in 1840, Richard Henry Dana described the town as "a small settlement directly before the fort, composed of about 40 dark-brown-looking huts or houses, and two larger ones plastered." Bostonian Mary Chase Walker, San Diego's first schoolhouse teacher, was more blunt: "Of all the dilapidated, miserable looking places I had ever seen this was the worst."

🔟 Coronado

Sometimes described as an island because its village-like atmosphere is far removed from the big city, picturesque Coronado lies on a sliver of land between the Pacific Ocean and San Diego Bay. More retired Navy officers live here than any other place in the US, and although the military presence is high, it's unobtrusive. For over 100 years, visitors have flocked to Coronado to be part of this charmed life. For even with its thriving resorts, restaurants, sidewalk cafés, and unique shops, the village never seems overwhelmed.

Dining alfresco at the Hotel del Coronado

🍴 Enjoy the Hotel del Coronado's ambience by sitting in the Babcock & Story Bar for a drink and tapas.

🚶 Excellent historical walking tours depart from Glorietta Bay Inn, 1630 Glorietta Blvd; (619) 435-5993; Wed at 2pm; Adm.

• Map C6
• www.coronado visitorcenter.com
• Hotel del Coronado: 1500 Orange Ave; (619) 435-6611; www.hoteldel.com
• Meade House: 1101 Star Park Cir
• Coronado Museum of History and Art: 1100 Orange Ave; (619) 435-7242; Open 9am–5pm Mon–Fri, 10am–5pm Sat–Sun; Suggested adm $4; www.coronado history.org
• Ferry Landing Market Place: 1201 First St at B Ave; (619) 435-8895; Open 10am daily, various closing times
• Coronado to San Diego Ferry: (619) 234-4111; Adm $4.25

Top 10 Attractions

1. Hotel del Coronado
2. Coronado Bridge
3. Mansions along Ocean Boulevard
4. Meade House
5. Silver Strand State Beach
6. Orange Avenue
7. Coronado Museum of History and Art
8. Ferry Landing Market Place
9. San Diego Ferry
10. Naval Air Station North Island & the US Naval Amphibious Base

Hotel del Coronado
A San Diego symbol, this 1887–88 Queen Anne wooden masterpiece *(right)* is a National Historic Landmark. This was the first hotel west of the Mississippi to be equipped with electric lights. Don't miss the photo gallery.

Coronado Bridge
Connecting San Diego to Coronado since 1969, this 2.2-mile (3.5-km) span *(below)* has won architectural awards for its unique design. Struts and braces hidden in a box girder give it a sleek look, and its blue color imitates the sky.

Mansions along Ocean Boulevard
Designed by prominent early 20th-century architects Hebbard and Gill, mansions *(above)* dominate Coronado's oceanfront.

Meade House
L. Frank Baum made Coronado his home in 1904 and produced much of his work while living at this charming house, now a private residence.

L. Frank Baum was the author of The Wonderful Wizard of Oz. Published in 1900, it was the first book in his Oz series.

Silver Strand State Beach
In 1890, John D. Spreckels *(see p39)* built bungalows and tents along the beach *(above)*. "Tent City" allowed all families to enjoy the once-exclusive beach. Today, anyone can come to dig for clams, beachcomb, and enjoy roasted hot dogs.

San Diego Ferry
Before the Coronado Bridge, access was only possible by a long drive around Southern San Diego or via the ferry. The ferry *(below)* is now only for passengers.

Naval Air Station North Island & the US Naval Amphibious Base
You might see navy planes flying overhead or Navy SEALS training on Silver Strand Beach. Lindbergh *(see p39)* began his flight across the Atlantic from here.

Orange Avenue
Coronado's main shopping street *(right)* is filled with elegant restaurants and sidewalk cafés, as well as a theater and a historical museum. Independence Day and Christmas parades bring residents out to celebrate in true hometown style.

Coronado Museum of History and Art
Housed in a distinctive 1910 Neo-Classical bank building, galleries exhibit Coronado's early history. Fascinating photos reveal the initial years of the Hotel del Coronado, Tent City, and the military.

Ferry Landing Market Place
Next to the ferry dock is a shopping area surrounded by walkways and benches offering harbor views. The shops sell beachwear, jewelry, souvenirs, and art. This is a handy spot to rent a bike or grab a snack.

The Duke & Duchess of Windsor
When the British King Edward VIII gave up his throne to marry American Wallis Simpson, romantics insisted they originally met at the Hotel del Coronado. In 1920, Wallis Spencer, then married to a naval officer of that name, lived at the hotel. That April, Edward visited Coronado as Prince of Wales. It is unclear whether the future couple actually met; it wasn't until 15 years later that they were formally introduced.

Point Loma

Point Loma was once one of the city's most rough-and-tumble areas. San Diego's first boats were tied up here, followed by the largest whaling operation on the West Coast and leather tanning and tallow production. Today, sailboats and yachts grace the marinas, and the waterfront homes make up some of the most expensive real estate in the city. The Cabrillo National Monument, the third most-visited monument in the US, boasts the most breathtaking views of the entire city.

Inscription at the base of
Cabrillo Statue

🖰 At the Cabrillo Monument Visitor Center, some vending machines offer snack food. But if you want to spend the day hiking the trails and exploring the tide pools, bring food and water with you.

✒ If it's a cloudy day, wait until the sun comes out to visit. Bring binoculars if you can, to enjoy the incredible views.

The San Diego Metropolitan Transit comes out to the monument. Take bus 28 or 84c from the Old Town Transportation Center.

- Map A6
- Cabrillo National Monument Visitor Center: 1800 Cabrillo Memorial Drive; (619) 557-5450; Open 9am–5pm daily; Adm $5 per vehicle; $3 per person (cyclists and walk-ins); tickets last for 7 days; www.nps.gov/cabr

Top 10 Sights

1. Cabrillo Statue
2. Old Point Loma Lighthouse
3. Visitor Center
4. Bayside Trail
5. Military Exhibit
6. Whale Overlook
7. Sunset Cliffs
8. Fort Rosecrans National Cemetery
9. Tide Pools
10. Point Loma Nazarene University

Cabrillo Statue

The actual spot where Cabrillo stepped ashore is on a spit of land downhill at Ballast Point. However, this magnificent statue *(right)* is a worthy tribute to the brave explorer and his men who ventured across uncharted seas to claim new territory for Spain.

Old Point Loma Lighthouse

This Cape Cod-style building *(right)* was completed in 1855. Unfortunately, coastal fog so often obscured the beacon light that another lighthouse, the New Point Loma Lighthouse, had to be built below the cliff.

Visitor Center

Park rangers are on hand to answer questions. Browse through the center's outstanding books about the Spanish, Native Americans, and early California, or enjoy the daily film screenings.

New Point Loma Lighthouse

Bayside Trail

A two-mile (3.2-km) round-trip hiking path winds along an old military defense road. Signs along the way help you identify indigenous plants such as sage scrub, lemonade berry, and Indian paintbrush.

Military Exhibit
After the 1941 Pearl Harbor attack, many felt that San Diego would be the next target. The exhibit explores how the military created a coastal defense system and the largest gun in the US.

Sunset Cliffs
A path runs along the edge of these spectacular 400-ft (122-m) high cliffs (above), but signs emphatically warn against their instability. Access the beach from Sunset Cliffs Park.

Tide Pools
Now protected by law, starfish, anemones, warty sea cucumbers and wooly sculpins thrive in their own little world.

Whale Overlook
Pacific gray whales migrate yearly to give birth in the warm, sheltered waters of Baja California before heading back to Alaska for a summer of good eating. January and February are the best times to spot whales (above).

Fort Rosecrans National Cemetery
The southern end of Point Loma belongs to the military installations of Rosecrans Fort. Innumerable crosses mark the graves (below) of 88,000 US veterans, some of whom died at the Battle of San Pasqual in the Mexican-American War.

Point Loma Nazarene University
Once a yoga commune, much of the original architecture of this Christian university (above) is still intact.

Juan Cabrillo

After participating in the conquest of Mexico and Guatemala, Juan Cabrillo was instructed to explore the northern limits of the West Coast of New Spain in search of gold, and to discover a route to Asia. He arrived at Ballast Point on September 28, 1542, claimed the land for the crown of Spain and named it San Miguel. Unfortunately, Cabrillo died only a few months later from complications of a broken bone. Spain considered the expedition a failure and left its new territory untouched for the next 225 years.

Mission Basilica San Diego de Alcalá

When Russian fur traders neared California in the 18th century, Spain knew it had to establish a presence in its half-forgotten territory. Founded by Father Junípero Serra in 1769, this was California's first mission. Serra encouraged Native Americans to live here, exchanging work in the fields for religious instruction. Harassment by soldiers and lack of water supplies caused the mission to be moved from its original location in Old Town to this site. In 1976, Pope Paul VI bestowed the mission with the status of minor basilica.

LA CASA DEL PADRE SERRA

Wall engraving at La Casa del Padre Serra

⊘ Food and drinks are not allowed inside the mission.

The San Diego Trolley stops a good three blocks away, so you should drive to the mission if walking is difficult.

- Map E3
- 10818 San Diego Mission Rd
- (619) 281-8449
- www.mission sandiego.com
- Open 9am–4:45pm daily
- Adm $3
- Tote-a-Tape Tours $2
- Church: Mass 7am & 5:30pm Mon–Fri, 5:30pm Sat, 7am, 8am, 9am, 10am, 11am, noon & 5:30pm Sun

Top 10 Sights

1. La Casa del Padre Serra
2. Church
3. Campanario
4. Cemetery
5. Garden Statues
6. Padre Luis Jayme Museum
7. Chapel
8. Gardens
9. Father Luis Jayme Memorial
10. El Camino Real

1 La Casa del Padre Serra
The original 1774 adobe walls and beams survived an Indian attack, a military occupation, earthquakes, and years of neglect. Padres lived simply and with few comforts.

3 Campanario
This 46-ft (14-m) bell-tower defines California mission architecture. One of the bells is considered an original, and the crown atop one bell signifies it was cast in a royal foundry.

2 Church
The width of a mission church was determined by the size of available beams. Restored to specifications of a former 1813 church on this site, the church *(above)* features adobe bricks, the original floor tiles, and wooden door beams.

4 Cemetery
Although it no longer contains real graves, this is considered the oldest cemetery *(below)* in California. The crosses are made of original mission tiles. A memorial honors Native Americans who died during the mission era.

5 Garden Statues

Four statues of St. Anthony of Padua *(right)*, patron saint of the Indians, Father Serra, St. Joseph, saint of Serra's expedition, and St. Francis oversee the inner garden.

6 Padre Luis Jayme Museum

Artifacts here include records of births and deaths in Father Serra's hand-writing, the last crucifix he held, and old photos showing the extent of the mission's dereliction prior to restoration efforts.

9 Padre Luis Jayme Memorial

On November 5, 1775, Indians attacked the mission. A cross *(below)* marks the approximate spot where Kumeyaay Indians killed Jayme, California's first martyr.

10 El Camino Real

Also called the Royal Road or the King's Highway, this road linked the 21 California missions, each a day's distance apart on foot.

7 Chapel

Taken from a Carmelite monastery in Plasencia, Spain, this small chapel *(below)* features choir stalls, a throne, and an altar dating from the 1300s. The choir stalls are held together by grooves, not nails. The raised seats allowed the monks to stand while singing.

8 Gardens

Exotic plants add to the lush landscaping surrounding the mission *(above)*. With few indigenous Californian plants available, missionaries and settlers introduced plants from all parts of the world, including cacti from Mexico and aloes and bird of paradise from South Africa.

Father Junípero Serra

Franciscan Father Junípero Serra spent 20 years in Mexico before arriving to establish a Spanish presence in California. Crossing the desert in what came to be called the "Sacred Expedition," the appalling conditions of the march left few survivors. But Serra, undeterred, established California's first mission in 1769. He founded nine missions by 1784.

TOP 10 SeaWorld

Starfish

SeaWorld's great black-and-white whale superstar Shamu is an identifiable San Diego icon, with 12,000 marine and aquatic animals serving as his extras. Opened in 1964, SeaWorld has grown into an internationally acclaimed attraction welcoming four million visitors a year. It also operates a center for oceanography and marine mammal research, and rehabilitates stranded and injured animals. Tropically landscaped grounds and educational exhibits provide respite from the constant action.

Visitors greeting SeaWorld's killer whales

🅞 The Shipwreck Reef Café offers the widest food selection in a fun ship-like setting.

⏱ When you enter, check the show times behind the park map and plan your day accordingly. Some presentations and shows occur only a few times a day.

Check the website for discount tickets and avoid long lines at the entrance.

• Map B4
• 500 SeaWorld Dr, Mission Bay
• (619) 226-3901
• Open 10am–5pm daily; on some weekends and in summer, opens at 9am and occasionally closes at 11pm
• Adm adult/child $73/$65
• Parking $15
• Guided tours $19/$42
• Several admission tickets to SeaWorld and other Southern California theme parks available
• www.seaworld.com/sandiego

Top 10 Attractions

1. Shamu Rocks
2. Blue Horizons
3. Penguin Encounter
4. Sea Lions Live
5. Sesame Street Bay of Play
6. Pets Rule!
7. Wild Arctic
8. Shipwreck Rapids
9. Shark Encounter
10. Journey to Atlantis

1 Shamu Rocks

Shamu and fellow killer whales perform with their trainers in this amazing night show filled with astonishing choreographed routines *(right)* set to rock and roll music, with multimedia elements and light effects.

2 Blue Horizons

Atlantic bottlenose dolphins *(below)*, and two 3,000-lb (1,361-kg) pilot whales leap, cavort, and dive to music. Enthusiastic trainers and acrobatic performers dance and dive with them in this lively and entertaining show.

3 Penguin Encounter

Penguins here live in an environment that re-creates conditions in Antarctica *(above)*. Twice a day, feeders come out to discuss penguin habits and answer your questions.

4 Sea Lions Live

Clyde and Seamore are two sea lions that perform wacky versions of popular TV shows with stagehand Biff.

Wear a hat and use sunblock; the sun can be intense if you're sitting on the bleachers watching a show.

Pacific Passage

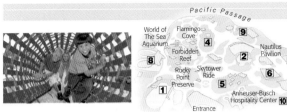

World of The Sea Aquarium 8
Flamingo Cove 4
Forbidden Reef
Rocky Point Preserve 1
Skytower Ride 5
9
2
6
Nautilus Pavilion 3
7
Anheuser-Busch Hospitality Center 10
Entrance

Sesame Street Bay of Play
Airbags, nets, and run-through tubes are ideal for active children *(above)*. Take a ride on Elmo's flying fish for fun on an imaginary ocean.

Shark Encounter
Learn to differentiate between a male and female shark as you step on a walkway with an underwater view *(below)* of several shark species.

Journey to Atlantis
An 8-passenger Greek fishing boat twists and drops unpredictably through mist and special effects while teaching you about the lost city of Atlantis.

Pets Rule!
Adorable dogs, cats, and other domestic animals take the stage in a backyard paradise where trees, a fence, and a pool are used as props for animals performing amusing stunts. A great show for all the family.

Shipwreck Rapids
If you aren't already wet enough, try a ride on Shipwreck Rapids, a 9-person raft-like inner tube that plunges down rapids and passes under bridges where, for a small fee, others can squirt water at you.

Animal Rescue Programs

Every year hundreds of stranded marine animals are rescued, treated, and released back into the wild by SeaWorld specialists. In 1997 a three-day-old whale weighing 1,500 lb (680 kg) was found off the California coast. Named J.J., the whale spent 15 months in rehabilitation at SeaWorld before she was successfully returned to the ocean. The knowledge gained by staff during the recovery period was shared worldwide.

Wild Arctic
Pretend you're on an expedition to the Arctic on a ride that simulates a jet copter landing. Walk past an above- and below-water tank to view white beluga whales and walruses, and don't miss the polar bear *(right)*.

You might want to carry an extra shirt in case you get wet from the rides and shows.

La Jolla

Only barren pueblo land in 1886, developer Frank Botsford bought a substantial area in La Jolla which he subdivided. Other real estate developers soon caught on to La Jolla's potential and built stylish resorts. But it wasn't until Ellen Browning Scripps arrived in 1896 with her generous civic endowments that the town developed as a research, education, and art center. Now, La Jolla sits on some of the most expensive real estate in the US. It's no wonder that residents refer to their slice of heaven as the "Jewel."

Torrey Pines State Reserve

● The café at the Museum of Contemporary Art serves a good range of tasty sandwiches and salads.

◐ Watch the paragliders launch from the Torrey Pines cliffs, or stroll the UCSD campus and its Stuart Collection.

• Map N2
• Museum of Contemporary Art: 700 Prospect; (858) 454-3541; Open 11am–5pm Fri–Thu; 11am–7pm 3rd Thu each month; Adm $10; Free 5–7pm Thu; www.mcasd.org
• Athenaeum Music & Arts Library: 1008 Wall St; (858) 454-5872; Open 10am–5:30pm Tue–Sat (to 8:30pm Wed); www.ljathenaeum.org
• Mount Soledad: Soledad Rd; Open 7am–10pm daily
• Scripps Institution of Oceanography: 8622 Kennel Way; http://sio.ucsd.edu
• University of California, San Diego: 9500 Gilman Dr; (858) 534-2230; www.ucsd.edu

Top 10 Attractions

1. Museum of Contemporary Art
2. Athenaeum Music & Arts Library
3. Ellen Browning Scripps Park
4. Mount Soledad Veterans Memorial
5. Birch Aquarium at Scripps
6. Scripps Institution of Oceanography
7. La Jolla Playhouse
8. Torrey Pines State Reserve
9. Salk Institute
10. University of California, San Diego (UCSD)

Museum of Contemporary Art

Only a fraction of more than 3,000 works from every noteworthy art movement since 1950 are on display at this renowned museum *(above)*.

Athenaeum Music & Arts Library

Although a membership is required to check out materials from this outstanding collection of music and art, you can attend music performances and visit its art exhibitions.

Coastal view of La Jolla

Ellen Browning Scripps Park

Stroll along palm-lined walkways and gaze out over panoramic coastline views *(below)*.

Mount Soledad Veterans Memorial

This memorial, erected in 1954 to honor Korean veterans, now honors veterans from all wars. Six walls beneath a 43-ft (13-m) high cross hold 2,400 plaques.

Maps of UCSD are available from the Information Booths at the campus entrances.

5 Birch Aquarium at Scripps

Brilliantly colored underwater habitats educate at this marine museum *(above)*. You'll feel like a scuba diver when viewing sharks swimming in an offshore kelp bed housed in a 70,000-gallon tank. Popular interactive exhibits reveal environmental changes happening now and predictions for the future *(see p53)*.

9 Salk Institute

Jonas Salk founded this institution *(see p44)* for biomedical research in 1960. Its scientists explore molecular biology, genetics, neurosciences, and plant biology.

Revelle College Dr
Scholars Drive South
Campus Loop

10 University of California, San Diego (UCSD)

Ten colleges make up one of the most prestigious public universities *(above)* in the country.

6 Scripps Institution of Oceanography

Leading the way in oceanographic research, this 1903 institute *(right)* is one of the world's largest. A part of UCSD, over 1,000 scientists at 18 centers are developing the latest marine technologies.

7 La Jolla Playhouse

Now part of UCSD's Mandell Weiss Center for the Performing Arts, the Play-house *(right)* features a state-of-the-art theater, rehearsal halls, and a restaurant *(see p50)*.

8 Torrey Pines State Reserve

At this gorgeous reserve *(see p46)*, hiking trails wind past coastal scrub, sculptured sandstone cliffs, wildflowers and woodlands, with stunning views of the Pacific. Guided tours leave from the visitor center.

Ellen Browning Scripps

Born in England in 1836, Scripps moved to the US in 1844. She became a teacher, investing her savings in her brother's news-paper ventures, the *Detroit Evening News* and the *Cleveland Press*. Already wealthy, she inherited a vast for-tune upon her brother's death in 1900. Scripps spent her last 35 years in La Jolla, giving away millions of dollars for the good of humanity. Her name now adorns countless schools, hospitals, research institutions, and parks.

TOP 10 Tijuana

The moment you step across "La Linea," as the border is called locally, the sensory assault is overwhelming: vendors, beggars, dust, souvenirs, music, and food smells are just the beginning. Leave the tourist zone and you'll find a city filled with some of the finest restaurants and cultural activities in Mexico and a community characterized by industriousness, resiliency, and resourcefulness.

Mural at Café La Especial

Cathedral de Nuestra Señora de Guadalupe

🍴 **Café La Especial, at Av Revolución & 3rd, #718, offers traditional Mexican fare.**

🚶 **A guided tour is a great way to visit Tijuana *(see p106).***

• Map E3
• www.tijuanaonline.org
• Centro Cultural de Tijuana: Paseo de los Héroes & Mina, Zona Rio; (664) 687-9600
• Frontón Jai Alai: Av Revolución & Calle 7
• Agua Caliente Racetrack: Blvd Agua Caliente 12027; (684) 682-3110
• Catedral de Nuestra Señora de Guadalupe: Calle 2a (Juarez) & Av Niños Heroes
• L.A. Cetto Cava: Av Cañon Johnson 2108; (664) 685-3031; Open 10am–5:30pm Mon–Fri; 10am–4pm Sat
• Parque Morelos: Blvd Insurgentes 16000; Open daily
• Museo de Cera: Calle 1, 8281; Open 10am–6pm daily; Adm US$1.50
• Plaza Monumental: Ave Pacifico 1, Playas de Tijuana; (664) 680-1808

Top 10 Attractions

1. Border Crossing
2. Avenida Revolución
3. Centro Cultural de Tijuana (Cecut)
4. Frontón Jai Alai
5. Agua Caliente Racetrack
6. Catedral de Nuestra Señora de Guadalupe
7. L.A. Cetto Cava
8. Parque Morelos
9. Museo de Cera
10. Plaza Monumental

Border Crossing
An estimated 60 million people pass through the world's busiest land border every year. While traffic snakes for miles to enter the US, entering Mexico takes less time.

Avenida Revolución
Bars, pharmacies, and souvenir shops embrace the tourist soul of Tijuana. Have your picture taken on the famous street corner with burros painted to look like zebras – an institution since 1954.

Tourists posing with burros

Centro Cultural de Tijuana (Cecut)
Classical music, dance, and traditional theater are performed here. In the same complex is the outstanding Museo de las Californias.

Frontón Jai Alai
Celebrities and the social elite once packed this Moorish palace to watch the fast-playing Jai Alai, a Basque game somewhat like squash. The landmark building *(left)* now hosts concerts and theater events.

USA
MEXICO

Agua Caliente Racetrack
Opened in 1929 as the Agua Caliente Spa & Casino, this greyhound racetrack *(above)* is all that's left of the famous complex that once attracted Hollywood celebrities.

Museo de Cera
Tijuana's wax museum presents 86 figures taken from the annals of American and Mexican history, art, and pop culture.

Plaza Monumental
At Plaza Monumental *(above)*, bullfighters from Mexico and Spain come to slay the bull in front of up to 25,000 aficionados. Day tours are available from San Diego.

L.A. Cetto Cava
The vineyards of Baja are Mexico's largest, and this winery welcomes visitors for tours. The spotless facility offers dozens of wines for tasting and purchase, as well as wine-related souvenir items.

Catedral de Nuestra Señora de Guadalupe
Tijuana's oldest church *(above)* has evolved from its humble 1902 origins. Domes top the towers and gold leaf adorns the barrel-vaulted interior.

Parque Morelos
This State Park is an ecological reserve with gardens, pedestrian walkways, and a small lake. The train ride and play areas make the park popular with families, especially on weekends, when there are clowns and puppet shows.

Tijuana's *Maquiladoras*

Tijuana's population is one of the fastest-growing in Mexico due in part to employment offered by scores of *maquiladora* factories that have sprung up. Taking advantage of low wages and close proximity to the US, workers at these foreign-owned plants assemble electronics, appliances, and TV sets. Wages are higher than elsewhere in Mexico, but so is the cost of living.

Many US car rental agencies do not allow their cars to be taken over the border. Buy Mexican car insurance before entering.

Left **Statue at Mission de Alcalá** Center **Mission Church** Right **Panama-California Exposition**

⑩ Moments in History

1 In the Beginning

A skull discovered in 1929 established human presence in San Diego about 12,000 years ago. The Kumeyaay Indians, present at the time of Cabrillo's landing, lived in small, organized villages. Hunters and gatherers, they subsisted on acorns, berries, and small prey.

2 Discovery by Juan Cabrillo (1542)

Cabrillo *(see p27)* was the first European to arrive at San Diego Bay. The Spanish believed that Baja and Alta California were part of a larger island, "Isla California," named after a legendary land in a popular Spanish 15th-century romance. California became part of the Spanish Empire for the next 279 years.

3 The Spanish Settlement (1769)

Fearing the loss of California, Spain sent an expedition, led by Gaspar de Portolá and Franciscan friar Junípero Serra *(see p29)*, to establish military posts and missions to Christianize the Indians. Disastrous for the Indians, the settlement survived and a city slowly took hold.

4 Mexico Gains Independence (1821)

After gaining independence, Mexico secularized the California missions and distributed their

Mexican flag

land to the politically faithful. The resulting rancho system of land management lasted into the 20th century. Without Spanish trade restrictions, ports were open to all and San Diego became a center for the hide trade.

5 California Becomes a State (1850)

The Mexican era only lasted until 1848. One bloody battle between the Americans and Californios *(see p40)* was fought at San Pasqual *(see p41)*. With a payment of $15 million and the treaty of Guadalupe Hidalgo, California became part of the US and then later its 31st state.

6 Alonzo Horton Establishes a New City (1867)

Horton realized an investment opportunity to develop a city closer to the water than Old Town. He bought 960 acres for $265, then sold and gave lots to anyone who could build a brick house. Property values soared, especially after a fire in 1872 in Old Town. "New Town" became today's San Diego.

7 Transcontinental Railroad Arrives (1885)

Interest was renewed in San Diego when the Transcontinental Railroad finally reached town. Real estate speculators poured in, infrastructure was built, and the future looked bright. However, Los Angeles appeared even more promising, and San Diego's population, which had risen from 5,000 to 40,000 in two years, shrank to 16,000.

8 Panama-California Exposition (1915–16)

To celebrate the opening of the Panama Canal and draw economic attention to the first US port of call on the West Coast, Balboa Park *(see pp14–15)* was transformed into a brilliant attraction. Fair animals found homes at the zoo *(see pp16–17)* and Spanish-Colonial buildings became park landmarks.

9 California-Pacific Exposition (1935–36)

A new Balboa Park exposition was launched to help alleviate effects of the Great Depression. The architect Richard Requa designed buildings inspired by Aztec, Mayan, and Pueblo Indian themes.

10 World War II

The founding of the aircraft industry, spurred by the presence of Ryan Aviation and Convair, gave San Diego an enduring industrial base. After Pearl Harbor, the headquarters of the Pacific Fleet moved here. The harbor was enlarged, and hospitals, camps, and housing transformed the city's landscape.

View from Balboa Park, 1916

Top 10 Famous San Diego Figures

1 Father Luis Jayme (1740–75)
California's first martyr died in an Indian attack *(see p29)*.

2 Richard Henry Dana (1815–82)
Author of the 19th-century classic *Two Years Before the Mast*, a historical record of early San Diego *(see p23)*.

3 William Heath Davis (1822–1909)
This financier *(see p8)* established a new settlement known as "Davis' Folly".

4 Alonzo Horton (1813–1909)
The "Father" of San Diego successfully established the city's present location in 1867.

5 Wyatt Earp (1848–1929)
The gunman *(see p8)* owned saloons and gambling halls in the Gaslamp Quarter.

6 John D. Spreckels (1853–1926)
A generous philanthropist, businessman *(see p25)*, and owner of Hotel del Coronado.

7 L. Frank Baum (1856–1919)
This author *(see p24)* lived in and considered Coronado an "earthly paradise."

8 Charles Lindbergh (1902–74)
The first to fly solo across the Atlantic in 1927 *(see p25)*.

9 Theodore Geisel (1904–91)
Best known as Dr. Seuss, he lived and worked in La Jolla.

10 The San Diego Chicken (b. 1953)
The chicken-suited antics of Ted Giannoulas have brought international attention to San Diego sports and events.

Dr. Seuss was the author of the children's classics The Cat in the Hat and Green Eggs and Ham.

Left **Victorian houses in Heritage Park** Right **Façade of Mission San Luis Rey de Francia**

🔟 Historic Sites

1 Ballast Point
In 1542, while Kumeyaay Indians waited on a beach at Ballast Point, Juan Cabrillo *(see p27)* stepped ashore and claimed the land for Spain. In 1803, the "Battle of San Diego Bay" took place here, after Spanish Fort Guijarros fired on an American brig in a smuggling incident.
⬥ *Map B6 • Point Loma*

2 Old Town
After Mexico won its independence from Spain in 1821, retired soldiers and their families moved downhill from the presidio, built homes, and opened businesses. An open trade policy attracted others to settle, and by the end of the decade, 600 people lived in Old Town – San Diego's commercial and residential center until 1872.

3 Presidio Hill
Spain established its presence in California atop this hill, and Father Serra founded the first mission *(see pp28–9)* here. During the Mexican-American War in 1846, possession of an earthwork fortress on the hill changed hands three times between the Americans and Californios. ⬥ *Map P5*

4 Mission Basilica San Diego de Alcalá
Originally built on Presidio Hill in 1769, this mission moved up the valley a few years later. The first of 21 missions, it was the

Gaslamp Quarter

birthplace of Christianity in California. It was the only mission to be attacked by Indians. In 1847, the US Cavalry occupied the grounds *(see pp28–9)*.

5 Gaslamp Quarter
Filled with late-19th-century Victorian architecture, this premier historic site was once the commercial heart of Alonzo Horton's *(see pp38–9)* New Town. When development moved north to Broadway, the neighborhood succumbed to gambling halls and brothels. It was revitalized in the 1970s *(see pp8–9)*.

6 Lindbergh Field
San Diego International Airport *(see p85)* is popularly called Lindbergh Field after Charles Lindbergh *(see p39)*, who began the first leg of his trans-Atlantic crossing from here in 1927. The US Army Air Corps drained the surrounding marshland, took over the small airport, and enlarged the runways to accommodate the heavy bomber aircraft manufactured in San Diego during World War II. ⬥ *Map C5*

⬅ *The Mexican-Californian ranchers were known as Californios.*

7 Border Field State Park

The Mexican-American War concluded with the signing of the Treaty of Guadalupe Hidalgo *(see p38)* on February 2, 1848. A US and Mexican Boundary Commission then determined the new international border between the two countries, with California divided into Alta and Baja. A marker placed in 1851 on a bluff in this park *(see p87)* marks the farthest western point of the new border. ◎ Map E3 • (619) 575-3613 • Call for opening hours

Memorial plaque at San Pasqual Valley

8 San Pasqual Battlefield State Historic Park

On December 6, 1846, an army of volunteer Mexican-Californian ranchers, known as Californios, defeated the invading American army of dragoons in one of the bloodiest battles of the Mexican-American War. Though the Californios won the battle, they subsequently lost the war, and California became part of the US. ◎ Map E2 • 15808 San Pasqual Valley Rd, Escondido • Open 8am–5pm Sat & Sun

9 Mission San Luis Rey de Francia

Nicknamed the "King of Missions" for its size, wealth, and vast agricultural estates, this mission is the largest adobe structure in California. The Franciscan padres Christianized 3,000 Indians here. After secularization, the mission fell into disrepair and was used for a time as military barracks. Now restored to its former glory, the Franciscan Order administers the mission *(see p95)*.

10 Julian

The discovery of gold in the hills northeast of San Diego in 1870 was the largest strike in Southern California. For five years miners poured into the town of Julian *(see p96)*, which would have become the new county seat if San Diego supporters had not plied the voters of Julian with liquor on election day. The gold eventually ran out, but not until millions of dollars were pumped into San Diego's economy. ◎ Map F2

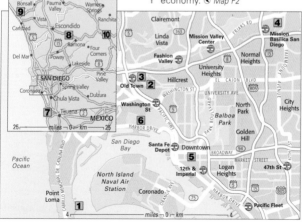

Left *Star of India* at the Maritime Museum Right Exhibits at the Chinese Historical Museum

🔟 Museums & Art Galleries

1 Museums of Balboa Park
Housed in stunning structures of Spanish-Colonial, Mayan, and Aztec designs that are architectural treasures in their own right, exhibits at these acclaimed museums constantly change, making Balboa Park *(see pp14–15)* a year-round attraction. Enjoy the exhibits of fine art, photography, aerospace, anthropology, model trains, and much more *(see pp18–19)*.

2 Museum of Contemporary Art
The most important contemporary art trends are presented at this museum. Docent-led tours, lectures, and special family nights make art accessible to all. The museum's flagship facility *(see p32)* is at the former oceanfront home of Ellen Browning Scripps *(see p33)*, with a satellite location downtown *(see pp72–3)*.

Chinese Historical Museum signs

3 Maritime Museum of San Diego
This museum pays tribute to the men and ships that so influenced the history and life of San Diego. Fascinating permanent and temporary exhibitions educate and entertain, while several anchored ships can be boarded and explored. ⊗ Map G3
• 1492 N. Harbor Dr • (619) 234-9153
• Open 9am–8pm daily • Adm
• www.sdmaritime.com

4 San Diego Chinese Historical Museum
Artifacts such as ceramics, bone toothbrushes, and old photographs document a fascinating slice of San Diego's history in this Spanish-style building that once served as a Chinese mission. Of note is the ornate bed that once belonged to a Chinese warlord. In the back garden is a koi pond. ⊗ Map J5 • 404 3rd Ave
• (619) 338-9888 • Open 10:30am–4pm Tue–Sat, noon–4pm Sun • Adm
• www.sdchm.org

5 Tasende Gallery
This gallery presents international contemporary artists. Discover the colorful works of Gaudi-influenced artist Niki de Saint Phalle, the pen-and-ink drawings of Mexico's José Luis Cuevas, the bronze sculptures of Britain's Lynn Chadwick, and the surrealist paintings of Chilean Roberto Matta. ⊗ Map N2 • 820 Prospect St, La Jolla • (858) 454-3691

6 Alcala Gallery
Early Californian Impressionist art is well represented here by the landscapes of Charles A. Fries, Selden Connor Gile, Maurice Braun, and many others. The gallery also specializes in ancient pre-Columbian art, Classical and Asian antiquities, and prints. ⊗ Map N3 • 950 Silverado St, La Jolla • (858) 454-6610

7 David Zapf Gallery

This fine arts gallery specializes in San Diego artists. Exhibitions feature paintings, drawings, photography, sculptures, and custom furniture from artists such as Mario Uribe, Gail Roberts, Paul Henry, and Johnny Coleman. The glowing, spiritual landscapes of Nancy Kittredge merit special notice. ◉ *Map H2* • *2400 Kettner Blvd* • *(619) 232-5004*

8 Michael J. Wolf Fine Arts

The oldest gallery in the Gaslamp Quarter features works of emerging US and international contemporary artists. Notice the colorful cubism of Stephanie Clair, the urban landscapes of Luigi Rocca, and the mixed media paintings of Josue Castro, who is inspired by the colors of the Zapotecan culture of Oaxaca. ◉ *Map K5* • *363 5th Ave* • *(619) 702-5388*

9 Joseph Bellows Gallery

This intimate gallery showcases important vintage prints and contemporary photographs. Three exhibition areas display photography of a superb quality, and host a busy program of themed group exhibitions, as well as solo shows. Both renowned and emerging photographers are represented, and past shows have included work by Ansel Adams, Maggie Taylor, and Bradford Washburn. ◉ *Map N3* • *7661 Girard Ave, La Jolla* • *(858) 456-5620*

Artist at the Spanish Village Art Center

10 Spanish Village Art Center

In a Spanish village-like atmosphere *(see p15)*, adobe houses from the 1935–36 California-Pacific Exposition have been transformed into delightful artists' studios, where you can shop or even take a lesson from the artists. ◉ *Map M1* • *(619) 233-9050* • *Open 11am–4pm daily* • *www.spanishvillageart.com*

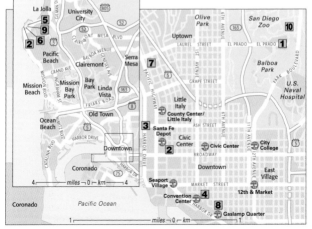

Left **San Diego County Administration Center** Right **Hotel del Coronado**

Architectural Highlights

1 San Diego County Administration Center

Four architects responsible for San Diego's look collaborated on this civic landmark. What began as a Spanish-Colonial design evolved into a more "Moderne" 1930s style with intricate Spanish tile work and plaster moldings on the tower. ◈ *Map H3 • 1600 Pacific Hwy • Open 8am–5pm Mon–Fri*

2 California Tower and Dome

Bertram Goodhue designed this San Diego landmark for the California-Panama Exposition of 1915–16, using Spanish Platform Platform Platform Plateresque, Baroque, and Rococo details. The geometric tile dome imitates Spanish Moorish ceramic work. An iron weather vane in the shape of a Spanish ship tops the 200-ft (61-m) tower *(see p15)*. ◈ *Map L1*

3 Mormon Temple

The temple of the Church of the Latter Day Saints is an ornate, futuristic structure. The golden trumpet-playing angel, Moroni, crowns one of the towers and points the way to Salt Lake City. Interiors are closed to the public. ◈ *Map B1 • 7474 Charmant Dr, La Jolla*

4 El Cortez

This landmark was once the tallest building and most famous hotel in

downtown San Diego. A glass elevator once led to the romantic Sky Room. Ornate Spanish details decorate the reinforced concrete structure, which is now a private condo building. ◈ *Map K3 • 702 Ash St*

5 Hotel del Coronado

Designed by James and Merritt Reid in 1887, this hotel was once the largest in the US to be built entirely of wood. Advanced for its time, the hotel had running bathroom water, telephones, and a birdcage elevator *(see p24)*. ◈ *Map C6*

6 Geisel Library

Named for famed children's author, Dr. Seuss *(see p39)*, and designed by William Pereira, tiers of glass walls are supported by reinforced concrete cantilevers. Filmmakers have used the library as a backdrop for sci-fi television shows. ◈ *Map B1 • UCSD: see p33*

7 Salk Institute

At one of the most famous buildings in San Diego *(see p33)*, twin six-story laboratories comprised of teak panels, concrete and glass stand across from each other, separated by a smooth marble courtyard with a channel of water running down the middle. Note architect Louis Kahn's use of "interstitial" space:

California Tower and Dome

The County Administration Center was designed by Louis Gill, Sam Hamill, Richard Requa, and William Templeton Johnson.

mechanical devices between floors can change laboratory configurations. ◎ Map B1 • 10010 N. Torrey Pines Rd • (858) 453-4100 • Open 8:30am–5pm Mon–Fri • www.salk.edu

Louis Bank of Commerce
Builders of the Hotel del Coronado, the Reid brothers can also take credit for one of the architectural treasures of the Gaslamp Quarter, a stately, four-story twin-towered Victorian structure (see p8). Built in 1888, it was San Diego's first granite building. Of special merit are the ornate bay windows that project from the façade. ◎ Map K5

Three colorful levels at Westfield Horton Plaza

Westfield Horton Plaza
Inside Westfield Horton Plaza is a wonderful hodgepodge of bridges and ramped walkways connecting six staggered levels, embellished with towers and cupolas. Its distinctive sherbet color scheme has been copied on many renovation projects throughout San Diego (see p48).

Cabrillo Bridge
Built as an entryway to the 1915–16 California-Panama Exposition, this cantilevered and multiple-arched bridge has a 1,500-ft (457-m) span. The best view of the bridge, especially during Christmas, is from the 163 Freeway below. ◎ Map K1

Top 10 Public Art Sights

Guardian of Water
A 23-ft (70-m) high granite sculpture depicts a pioneer woman. ◎ Map H3

Westfield Horton Plaza Fountain
Flowing water and electric lights were technological breakthroughs in 1909. Plaques honor city notables. ◎ Map J5

Tunaman's Memorial
A bronze sculpture of three tunamen casting their lines. ◎ Map B5

Murals at Chicano Park
Pylons of the Coronado Bridge are canvasses for 40 murals exploring Hispanic history. ◎ Map D5

The Cat in the Hat
The Cat in the Hat looks over Dr. Seuss' shoulder in this bronze sculpture. ◎ Map B1

Surfhenge
Towering surfboards stand in tribute to the surf gods. ◎ Map E3 • Imperial Beach Pier

Woman of Tehuantepec
A 1,200-lb (544-kg) piece of limestone is sculpted into an Indian woman. ◎ Map L2 • House of Hospitality

Sun God
A fiberglass bird stretches its wings atop a 15-ft (5-m) concrete arch. ◎ Map B1

Paper Vortex
A paper airplane is artfully transformed into an Origami crane. ◎ Map C5 • San Diego International Airport

Homecoming
A bronze sculpture depicts a sailor, wife, and child in a joyous homecoming embrace. ◎ Map G4 • Navy Pier, Harbor Drive

Left **Balboa Park's Alcázar Garden** Right **Ellen Browning Scripps Park**

Gardens & Nature Reserves

Balboa Park
This landmark destination and heart of San Diego offers an array of superb activities. Visit its gardens and museums for inspiration, to play sports, or to watch a concert. Although crowded, Sundays are good days to experience the community at leisure *see pp14–15).*

Mission Bay Park
This aquatic wonderland offers every watersport conceivable. You can also bicycle, play volleyball, jog, or nap on the grass. Excellent park facilities include boat rentals, playgrounds, fire rings, and picnic tables. ◉ Map B3 • 2688 E. Mission Bay Dr

Fountain at Balboa Park

Ellen Browning Scripps Park
Broad lawns shaded by palms and Monterrey cypress trees stretch the cliffs from La Jolla Cove to Children's Pool *(see p53).* Visitors can walk along promenades that offer a stunning view of the cliffs and beach of Torrey Pines. ◉ Map N2

Mission Trails Regional Park
At one of the country's largest urban parks, hiking and biking trails wind along rugged hills and valleys. The San Diego River cuts through the middle, and a popular trail leads to the Old Mission

Dam. The energetic can hike up Cowles Mountain, San Diego's highest peak at 1,591 ft (485 m). ◉ Map F3 • 1 Father Junípero Serra Trail

Los Peñasquitos Canyon Preserve
Archeologists discovered artifacts of the prehistoric La Jolla culture in this ancient canyon. You can also explore the adobe home of San Diego's first Mexican land grant family. Between two large coastal canyons, trails lead past woodland, oak trees, chaparral, and a waterfall. ◉ Map E2 • 12020 Black Mountain Rd

Kate O. Sessions Memorial Park
Named in honor of the mother of Balboa Park *(see p19),* this peaceful spot, with a terrific view of Mission Bay *(see p64),* is a popular picnicking area. Take advantage of the ocean breezes to rediscover kite flying. Walking trails extend 2 miles (3 km) through a canyon lined with native coastal sage. ◉ Map B3 • 5115 Soledad Rd, Pacific Beach

Torrey Pines State Reserve
A stretch of California's wild coast *(see p33)* offers a glimpse into an ancient ecosystem. Wildflowers bloom alongside hiking trails that lead past rare Torrey pines and 300 other endangered species. Viewing platforms

Torrey Pines State Reserve

overlook sandstone cliffs to the beach below. Spot quail, mule deer, and coyotes. ✎ *Map A1 • 12600 N. Torrey Pines Rd • (858) 755-2063 • Open 8am–sunset daily • Parking fee $10*

Spreckels Park
Named after John D. Spreckels (*see p39*), who donated the land, the park hosts Sunday concerts during the summer as well as art and garden shows. An old-fashioned bandstand, shady trees, green lawns, and picnic tables complete the picture of a small-town community center. ✎ *Map C6 • Coronado*

Embarcadero Marina Park
Join the downtown workers for some fresh air and sunshine. Wide grassy areas and benches give you solitude to enjoy the sweeping views of the harbor. During summer, concerts are held on the lawn. ✎ *Map J6 • Marina Park Way*

Tijuana River National Estuarine Research Reserve
Serene hiking paths meander through fields of wildflowers and native plants. More than 300 species of migratory birds stop by at different times of the year. A visitor center offers information to enhance your visit. ✎ *Map E3 • 301 Caspian Way, Imperial Beach*

Top 10 Spectacular Views

1 Point Loma
The breathtaking view from the peninsula's end takes in the city, harbor and Pacific Ocean (*see pp26–7*).

2 Coronado Bridge
Coronado, downtown, and San Diego harbor sparkle both day and night. ✎ *Map C6*

3 Mount Soledad
San Diego's most glorious view takes in Coronado, Point Loma, downtown, the valleys, and Mission Bay. ✎ *Map A2*

4 Bertrand at Mr. A's
Planes on approach to Lindbergh Field make dining a visual affair (*see p54*).

5 Manchester Grand Hyatt San Diego
The 40th-floor lounge offers views of San Diego Bay and Coronado (*see p114*).

6 Torrey Pines State Reserve
The view down the wind-eroded cliffs and across the Pacific is magnificent.

7 La Valencia Hotel
A drink on the terrace, overlooking vistas stretching to Torrey Pines, makes the world right (*see p115*).

8 Flying into San Diego
You can almost see what people are having for dinner as you fly in directly over downtown San Diego.

9 Presidio Park
A panoramic view extends from the freeways in Mission Valley below to Mission Bay and the Pacific (*see p80*).

10 Ferries in San Diego Harbor
On a sunny day nothing beats a ferry ride on the harbor, gazing at the white sailboats against a blue sky.

San Diego's Top 10

Westfield Horton Plaza

🔟 Stores & Shopping Centers

Westfield Horton Plaza
Macy's and Nordstrom department stores serve as anchors to this festive shopping experience, a destination in its own right. Designed as an amusement park for shoppers, ramps lead past staggered shopping levels that hold more than 130 specialty shops, a few restaurants, and movie theaters. The Plaza's landmark is the 1907 Jessop's Clock, a 21-ft (6.4-m) high timepiece with 20 dials that display the time in all parts of the world *(see p71)*. ⊗ *Map J5 • 4th Ave & Broadway • (619) 239-8180*

Nordstrom
Holding an almost cult-like status among shopping fanatics, "Nordies" remains as popular as ever for its vast clothing selection and impressive shoe department. Belying the plush surroundings, this department store can be quite affordable. Of course, there is always the personal shopper who will help you out in the designer section. The Nordstrom Café is popular for lunch, serving soups, sandwiches, pasta dishes, and salads. ⊗ *Map J5 • 103 Horton Plaza*

Le Travel Store
Since 1976, travelers Bill and Joan Keller have directed their passion for the road into a one-stop travel shop that offers anything a traveler might desire: Eagle Creek and Rick Steves luggage and backpacks, an array of packing organizers and travel accessories, and a good assortment of maps and guidebooks. ⊗ *Map J5 • 745 4th Ave • (619) 544-0005*

Bookstar
For nearly 50 years, the Loma Movie Theater presented Hollywood's greatest epics. In 1990, the theater was transformed into a grand bookstore. Well-stocked shelves sit on various levels as the floor steps down toward the former screen; the original ceiling still exists; and the carpet was specially milled to match the original. Bookstar is part of the Barnes & Noble chain. ⊗ *Map B4 • 3150 Rosecrans Pl • (619) 225-0465*

The Wine Bank
A regular clientele of wine connoisseurs frequent this intimate Gaslamp business. Hundreds of offerings from California and the rest of the world are found on two floors. The expertise of its wine professionals will help in your selection of fine wines in all price ranges. Call for the latest wine tasting schedule. ⊗ *Map K6 • 363 5th Ave • (619) 234-7487*

Sport Chalet
To participate in San Diego's outdoor life, you might need some sports equipment or active sportswear. This store, well located near Mission Bay, offers everything possible, including rentals of camping

Sign up for DK's email newsletter on traveldk.com

Shops at Seaport Village

equipment, kayaks, waterskis, and tennis racquets, as well as a full-service bike shop. You can also take scuba lessons or book a dive charter boat. ◈ Map B4
• 3695 Midway Dr • (619) 224-6777

Seaport Village

If you're looking for souvenirs or that unusual knick-knack for the shelf, this is the right place. You'll find kites, magnets, gifts for left-handed people, and t-shirts galore. The Village's superb location along San Diego's waterfront will keep you occupied. ◈ Map H5 • 849 W. Harbor Dr • (619) 235-4014 • Open 10am–9pm Sep–May; 10am–10pm Jun–Aug

Girard Avenue & Prospect Street

These intersecting streets in La Jolla are synonymous with upscale shopping and high-end art galleries. If you're seeking an expensive look, chic clothing boutiques and Italian shoe stores will happily oblige. The gorgeous displays in the home decor shops will give you great ideas to take home. In the

breezy arcades, don't miss the one-of-a-kind shops and beach-wear boutiques. ◈ Map N2

Fashion Valley

This ritzy shopping center contains six major department stores, including Neiman Marcus, Saks Fifth Avenue, and Nordstrom, as well as 200 specialty boutiques that carry just about everything. Tiffany & Co., MAC cosmetics, and Louis Vuitton are just a few of the specialty stores found here. The San Diego Trolley conveniently stops in the parking lot. ◈ Map C4 • 7007 Friars Rd

Mission Valley Center

Loehmann's, Nordstrom Rack, and Macy's Home & Furniture are just a few of the stores that carry items seen at higher-priced department stores. Budget shoppers flock to Target, Bed, Bath & Beyond, and more than 130 other stores. Don't confine your shopping to the center: across the street is Saks Off Fifth Avenue's outlet store. ◈ Map D4 • 1640 Camino del Rio N.

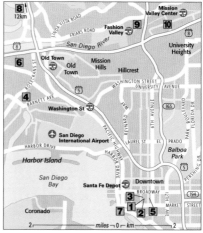

Left **The Old Globe** Right **Posters at La Jolla Playhouse**

🔟 Performing Arts Venues

1 The Old Globe
About 250,000 people annually attend top-rated performances at these three theaters in the same complex: the 600-seat Old Globe Theatre; the intimate, state-of-the-art Sheryl and Harvey White Theatre; and the outdoor Lowell Davies Festival Theatre *(see p14)*. 🔍 Map L1 • (619) 234-5623 • Tours 10:30am Sat & Sun • Adm • www.theoldglobe.org

2 Starlight Bowl
The San Diego Civic Light Opera performs summer Broadway shows in this idyllic Balboa Park setting *(see pp14–15)*. Although under the flight path of San Diego's International Airport, plane-spotters cue the performers when to freeze. Audiences good-humoredly accept the interruptions as part of the experience. 🔍 Map L2 • (619) 232-7827 • www.starlighttheatre.org

3 La Jolla Playhouse
Gregory Peck, Mel Ferrer, and Dorothy McGuire founded this acclaimed theater in 1947. All the Hollywood greats once performed here. Now affiliated with UCSD, many plays that debuted here have gone on to win the Tony; the theater itself took America's Outstanding Regional Theater award in 1993. 🔍 Map B1 • La Jolla Village Dr at Torrey Pines Rd, UCSD Campus, La Jolla • (858) 550-1010

4 Lyceum Theatre
Two theaters are part of the San Diego Repertory Theatre complex: the 550-seat Lyceum and the 270-seat Lyceum Space Theatre. Productions run from the experimental to multilingual performances and Shakespeare with a modern slant. In addition, the theater hosts visiting companies and art exhibitions. 🔍 Map J4 • 79 Horton Plaza • (619) 544-1000

5 Theatre in Old Town
Only 250 amphitheater-style seats wrap around the stage of this intimate theater housed in an Old Town barn. See dramas, musicals, and comedies such as *The History Boys*, *A Little Night Music*, and *A Christmas Carol*. 🔍 Map P5 • 4040 Twiggs St • (619) 337-1525

6 Copley Symphony Hall
Formerly known as the Fox Theatre, a Rococo-Spanish Renaissance extravaganza built in 1929, it was to be destroyed until developers donated it to the San Diego Symphony in 1984. Now brilliantly restored, the hall hosts excellent classical music concerts. 🔍 Map K4 • 750 B St • (619) 235-0804

La Jolla Playhouse sign

7 Spreckels Theatre
Commissioned by John D. Spreckels *(see p25)*, this Neo-Baroque downtown landmark presents theatrical productions and concerts. Murals, Classical

Spreckels Theatre sign

statuary, and an elegant marble lobby give the theater an aura of old San Diego. ◈ *Map J4 • 121 Broadway • (619) 235-9500*

San Diego Civic Theatre
If you missed the latest Broadway show, chances are the touring company will perform at this grand theater. Featuring local talent and the world's most acclaimed stars, the San Diego Opera stages four annual productions here. The California Ballet also perform here. ◈ *Map J4 • 1100 3rd Ave • (619) 570-1100*

Cricket Wireless Amphitheatre
Major pop artists perform from March to October in this acoustically notable open-air amphitheater. Great sight lines and giant video screens ensure a good view. Seating holds 10,000 people with another 10,000 on the grass. ◈ *Map E3 • 2050 Entertainment Cir, Chula Vista • (619) 671-3600*

Humphrey's Concerts by the Bay
From May to October, well-known performers of jazz, rock, comedy, blues, folk, and world music perform in an outdoor 1,350-seat amphitheater next to San Diego Bay. Special packages to Humphrey's Restaurant and Humphrey's Half Moon Bay Inn are available to patrons *(see p117)*. ◈ *Map B5 • 2241 Shelter Island Dr, Shelter Island • (619) 224-3577*

Top 10 Movies Filmed in San Diego

Citizen Kane, 1941
Orson Welles used the California Tower and Dome *(see p15)* in Balboa Park as Xanadu.

Sands of Iwo Jima, 1949
John Wayne raced up a hill at Camp Pendleton, the setting for the World War II battle.

Some Like It Hot, 1959
The distinctive structure of the Hotel del Coronado *(see p24)* formed a backdrop for Marilyn Monroe, Jack Lemmon, and Tony Curtis.

MacArthur, 1971
San Diego's own Gregory Peck is the general on Silver Strand State Beach *(see p64)*.

The Stunt Man, 1980
This Peter O'Toole film had stuntmen jumping off the roof of the Hotel del Coronado.

Top Gun, 1986
Tom Cruise chatted up Kelly McGillis at the iconic Kansas City Barbecue, in the harbor district.

Titanic, 1996
Filmed in an enormous, specially built water tank at Rosarito Beach, Mexico.

Almost Famous, 1999
Nothing much had to be changed from the Volkswagen and Birkenstock look of 1970s Ocean Beach *(see p64)*.

Pearl Harbor, 2000
Kate Beckinsale proved her love for Ben Affleck by coming to bid him goodbye at the San Diego Railroad Museum in Campo.

Traffic, 2000
Along with scenes of San Diego and Tijuana, *Traffic's* car explosion took place in the judges' parking lot of the Hall of Justice.

Left **Miniature town built from lego bricks at Legoland** Right **Roller coaster at Belmont Park**

Children's Attractions

1 San Diego Zoo

At the renowned San Diego Zoo, kids shriek in delight over the latest creepy-crawly in Bugtown, and build crafts at the animal-themed events. During seasonal holidays and summer, Dr. Zoolittle presents his entertaining science shows. The zoo also offers summer camps and art classes (see pp16–17).

Costumed characters at the zoo

2 SeaWorld

Kids love to press their faces against glass tanks, inches away from whales, sharks, and manatees. And there's nothing more fun than to be drenched by a performing dolphin (see pp30–31).

3 Reuben H. Fleet Science Center

Science can be fun for all. At Kid City, children aged 2–5 can play with conveyor belts, air chutes, and colorful foam blocks. Older kids go wild building complex structures at Block Busters! and enjoy other hands-on areas. In the Virtual Zone, kids can explore symmetry in time as a video camera records movement. ◈ Map M1 • (619) 238-1233 • Open 10am–7pm daily (to 8pm Sat) • Adm • www.rhfleet.org

4 Legoland

Children are fascinated by the 30 million plastic bricks fashioned into famous landmarks, life-sized African animals, and landscapes. In Fun Town, kids can drive real electric cars or pilot a helicopter; at the Imagination Zone, they can build race cars and robots. Magicians, ventriloquists, and puppeteers add to the fun. ◈ Map D1 • 1 Legoland Dr, Carlsbad • (760) 918-5346 • Adm

5 Children's Discovery Center at the San Diego Museum of Man

Located on the museum's second floor, kids dress up as pharaohs and learn about ancient Egypt by building a pyramid, deciphering hieroglyphics, and listening to the god Anubis explain the mummification process. At a re-creation of an archeological dig, children dig through sand for treasure and also learn about dating artifacts (see p18).

6 Belmont Park

This old-fashioned fun zone keeps the kids entertained for hours. They can take a ride on the Giant Dipper roller coaster, Tilt-a-Whirl, and an antique carousel; enjoy the Bumper Cars; or climb high above the ground on the challenging Sky

Dr. Zoolittle is the wacky resident scientist at San Diego Zoo.

Ropes Adventure. If you want to get wet, try The Plunge, a 175-ft (53-m) indoor pool *(see p60)*. ⊛ *Map A4 • 3190 Mission Blvd • (858) 488-1549 • Adm for rides*

Harbor Seal-Watching at Children's Pool

Children used to swim at this sheltered cove, but harbor seals had much the same idea. The seals are protected by federal law so the beach is now closed, and children must view the entertaining crowds of marine animals swimming and sleeping from behind a rope. ⊛ *Map N2 • Coast Blvd & Jenner St, La Jolla*

Marie Hitchcock
Puppet Theatre

Marie Hitchcock Puppet Theatre in Balboa Park

Named after the park's beloved "puppet lady" who delighted audiences with her magical skills, the Balboa Park Puppet Guild entertains kids and adults alike with a wonderful collection of marionettes and hand, rod, and shadow puppets. The Magic of Ventriloquism, Pinocchio, and Grimm's fairytale classics are some of the shows presented. ⊛ *Map L2 • Balboa Park • (619) 544-9203 • Adm • www.balboaparkpuppets.com*

San Diego Zoo Safari Park

This park has a large number of wild and endangered animals from Africa, Europe, Asia, North and South America, and Australia. Herds of animals roam freely in enclosures that replicate their natural habitats. Compatible animals are mixed, allowing visitors to observe their interactions. Children can enjoy the Petting Kraal and seeing the newborns at the Animal Care Center. Those over 8 can accompany their parents on a photo caravan for an encounter with giraffes and rhinos *(see p95)*.

Birch Aquarium at Scripps

Coral reefs, seahorses, octopi, and undulating jellyfish have a high ooh-and-ah factor for kids. The aquarium *(see p33)* presents special hands-on activities, scavenger hunts, craft work-shops, and slumber parties throughout the year, among more than 30 tanks filled with brilliantly colored fish. Guided tide-pool adventures for tots, seasonal whale-watching, and grunion runs take place off site. ⊛ *Map Q1 • 2300 Expedition Way • (858) 534-3474 • Open 9am–5pm daily • Adm • www.aquarium.ucsd.edu*

Animals living in harmony at the San Diego Zoo Safari Park

Grunion are small, silvery fish that beach themselves in the thousands to procreate at night, attracting large human crowds.

Left **Interior of Costa Brava** Right **Rooftop terrace at El Agave Tequileria**

Restaurants

Costa Brava
The aromas of authentic Spanish cooking will fire up your appetite on entering this restaurant. Sit under minimal whitewashed walls at the bar or outside, and savor the best tapas in San Diego. Guitarists, dancers, and satellite feeds of Spanish football entertain on occasion. ◈ *Map B3 • 1653 Garnet Ave • (858) 273-1218 • $$$*

Bertrand at Mr. A's
For casually elegant dining with a dazzling city view, this restaurant with friendly, attentive staff is hard to beat. The seasonal menu of American dishes is inspired by contemporary French-Mediterranean cuisine. Popular choices include sautéed Alaskan halibut with scallops and a trio of vegetarian creations. ◈ *Map J1 • 2550 5th Ave, 12th Floor • (619) 239-1377 • $$$$*

El Agave Tequileria
Ancient Mexican and Spanish spices and traditions make for a unique Mexican dining experience. Shrimp, sea bass, and the filet mignon prepared with goat's cheese and a dark tequila sauce are heavenly. Mole, the distinctive blending of spices, garlic, and sometimes chocolate, is a specialty, as well as 150 tequila selections. ◈ *Map P6 • 2304 San Diego Ave • (619) 220-0692 • $$$*

Cuervo Gold Especial Tequila

The Marine Room
Dine on exciting, romantic global cuisine derived from French classics. If you're not that hungry and would like to enjoy the sunset, try hors d'oeuvres in the lounge. ◈ *Map P2 • 2000 Spindrift Dr, La Jolla • (866) 644-2351 • $$$$$*

The Prado Restaurant
Hand-painted ceilings, glass sculptures, and whimsical artwork adorn this atmospheric restaurant. A large terrace overlooks the gardens of Balboa Park. A variety of margaritas and drinks from around South America complement an excellent cuisine best described as Latin and Italian fusion. ◈ *Map L1 • 1549 El Prado, Balboa Park • (619) 557-9441 • $$$*

The Fish Market
Take your pick from the "catch of the day" board and settle in at the oyster and sushi bar to await your table. Try for a coveted one on the outside deck directly over the water. You can request your fish be prepared grilled, fried, or Cajun style. A popular display counter offers fish to go. ◈ *Map G5 • 750 N. Harbor Dr • (619) 232-3474 • $$$$*

Baci Ristorante
Classic Italian cuisine is attentively presented in this subtly modern restaurant with Old World charm. The menu

Unless otherwise stated, all restaurants are open daily, accept credit cards, serve vegetarian meals, and provide disabled access.

Interior of The Prado Restaurant

includes creative daily specials, as well as traditional veal, seafood, and pasta dishes. The wine list is extensive. ◎ Map B3 • 1955 W. Morena Blvd • (619) 275-2094 • $$$

Asti Ristorante
Choose from a diverse menu that includes a wide range of homemade pasta dishes, accompanied by an extensive wine list. The warm ambience, child-friendly atmosphere, and generous portions make this restaurant a favorite with the locals. ◎ Map J5 • 728 5th Ave • (619) 232-8844 • $$$

Filippi's Pizza Grotto
At this Little Italy favorite, the dim lights, the red-checkered tablecloths, and hundreds of Chianti bottles hanging from the ceiling haven't changed in decades. Enter through the Italian deli in front to get to the spaghetti and meatballs and hand-tossed pizzas. ◎ Map H3 • 1747 India St • (619) 232-5095 • $

Emerald Chinese Seafood Restaurant
San Diego's best Chinese restaurants are found in Kearny Mesa. The Asian community packs into this large dining room to enjoy lunchtime dim sum and fresh, simple but exquisitely prepared seafood dishes at dinner. ◎ Map D3 • 3709 Convoy St, Kearny Mesa • (858) 565-6888 • $$$$

Top 10 Romantic Restaurants

Sky Room
Intimate tables and a view of the Pacific complement the sophisticated California cuisine. ◎ La Valencia Hotel (see p115).

1500 Ocean
Excellent service and elegant presentations at this impressive spot (see p91).

Chez Loma
Delicious French cuisine creates the ingredients for romance (see p91).

Old Venice
A casually elegant venue that's not too pricey in Point Loma. ◎ Map A6 • 2910 Cañon St • (619) 222-5888 • $$$$

BiCE
Authentic Italian dishes are served in this modern, elegant restaurant, ideal for a romantic supper. ◎ Map J5 • 425 Island Ave • (619) 239-2423 • $$$$

de' Medici
Enjoy a quiet and romantic meal, with Italian classics such as osso bucco and penne alla Bolognese. ◎ Map J5 • 815 5th Ave • (619) 702-7228 • $$$$

Candelas
Mexican nouvelle cuisine in a hacienda ambience. Seafood is a specialty. ◎ Map J5 • 416 3rd Ave • (619) 702-4455 • $$$$

The Marine Room
Haute cuisine, candlelight, and soft music arouse the senses (see p54).

George's at the Cove
More wedding proposals take place at this superb restaurant than anywhere else in San Diego (see p101).

Island Prime
Enjoy seafood, decadent desserts, and harborside views. ◎ Map C5 • 880 Harbor Island Dr • (619) 298-6802 • $$$$

For a key to price categories see p77.

Left **Interior of La Sala** Right **Façade of Corvette Diner**

🔟 Cafés & Bars

1 Café Bassam

An eclectic assortment of paintings, furnishings, and antiques decorates the walls of this Bankers Hill café. Order your special brew of espresso or tea and take it to a table to watch the world pass by. Glass jars hold over 100 different types of tea and coffee for sale. ⊗ Map K1 • 3088 5th Ave • (619) 808-3714

2 La Sala

Sitting in the hotel's lobby lounge amid Spanish mosaics, hand-painted ceilings and murals, red-tiled floors, and huge palms is like being in a Spanish palace. Order a drink and gaze out at the ocean; a pianist performs in the evening. On sunny days, take advantage of the outside tables. ⊗ Map N2 • La Valencia Hotel: See p115 • No dis. access

3 Lestat's Coffee House

Named after the character in Anne Rice's best-selling vampire novels, this café serves excellent coffee and pastries 24 hours a day. In the heart of increasingly hip Normal Heights, local bands entertain in the evening. Bring your laptop to enjoy a free Wi-Fi connection. ⊗ Map D4 • 3343 Adams Ave • (619) 282-0437

4 The Field

Literally imported from Ireland, the wood walls, flooring, decorations, and assorted curios were shipped over and reassembled. Even the bartenders and waitresses are the real thing, not to mention the Guinness. Grab a sidewalk seat on Fifth Avenue or try for a window seat upstairs. The pub food is great, too. ⊗ Map K5 • 544 5th Ave • (619) 232-9840

5 Top of the Hyatt

Window seats at this bar in the Manchester Grand Hyatt Hotel are at a premium during sunset, when people come to enjoy the breathtaking views of the bay, Coronado, Point Loma, and the jets over Lindbergh Field. Dark woods exude a sedate, plush atmosphere, with drink prices to match (see p114).

6 The Yard House

Whether you'd like a Kona Brewing Fire Rock or a Mad River Jamaican Red Ale, there's definitely a drink for you among the 130 featured beers and ales. Order by the half pint or half yard with some upscale appetizers. Music and TV sports events make the atmosphere young and noisy. ⊗ Map J4 • 1023 4th Ave • (619) 233-9273 • No dis. access

7 Beach at W Hotel

The ultimate in cool, this spot is the next best thing if you can't make it to the beach. Relax under the stars outside on comfortable banquette seating, order a martini and dig your toes into the heated sand, or go for a Mai Tai in a private, candlelit cabana. ⊗ Map H4 • 421 W. B St • (619) 398-3100 • No dis. access

Unless otherwise stated, all restaurants are open daily, accept credit cards, serve vegetarian meals, and provide disabled access.

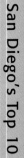

San Diego's Top 10

W Hotel

Twiggs Bakery & Coffee House

Enjoy a latte and a snack in this fun café. It's packed all day with neighborhood residents. On the second and fourth Mondays of each month, you'll find live poetry readings being held here. ⊗ *Map D4 • 4590 Park Blvd • (619) 296-0616*

Martinis Above Fourth

Located in central Hillcrest is this upscale Martini bar and cabaret piano lounge offering an extensive list of Martinis in the cocktail bar and the outdoor chill-out area. It also serves creative dishes such as pork chops with strawberry compote, while the live entertainment is excellent. ⊗ *Map C4 • 3940 4th Ave, Suite 200 • (619) 400-4500 • Closed Mon, Sun*

Corvette Diner

James Dean photos, neon, and 1950s road-trip artifacts adorn this diner's walls; burgers are named Kookie and Eddie; and a shiny Corvette sits as a shrine in this retro Hillcrest hangout. Libations from the full bar help dull the sensory onslaught. ⊗ *Map C4 • 2965 Historic Decatur Rd • (619) 542-1476*

Top 10 Breakfast Spots

Café 222
Try the pumpkin waffles and French toast here. ⊗ *Map J5 • 222 Island Ave • (619) 236-9902 • $*

Brockton Villa
Start the morning with crêpes, omelets, or a "tower of bagel" *(see p100).*

Crown Room
The room is a living legend, the Sunday feast amazing. ⊗ *Map C6 • Hotel del Coronado (see p115).*

Hash House A Go Go
Locals vote this the best breakfast spot in town. ⊗ *Map C4 • 3628 5th Ave • (619) 298-4646 • No dis. access • $*

Hob Nob Hill
Waffles, omelets and pancakes. ⊗ *Map J2 • 2271 1st Ave • (619) 239-8176 • $*

Broken Yoke Café
Choose from 30 varieties of omelets. ⊗ *Map A3 • 1851 Garnet Ave • (858) 270-0045 • $*

Kono's Café
Join the line for banana pancakes and breakfast burritos. ⊗ *Map A3 • 704 Garnet Ave • (858) 483-1669 • No credit cards • No dis. access • $*

Primavera Pastry Caffe
Croissants and three-egg omelets on sidewalk tables. ⊗ *Map C6 • 956 Orange Ave, Coronado • (619) 435-4191 • $*

The Cottage
Enjoy the freshly-baked cinnamon rolls and Belgian waffles *(see p101).*

The Mission
Breakfast is served until 3pm in this funky "Chino-Latino" café. ⊗ *Map A3 • 3795 Mission Blvd • (858) 488-9060 • $*

For a key to price categories see p77.

Left **Exterior of The Bitter End** Right **Interior of Croce's**

Nightlife

The Bitter End
Three floors cater to singles on the move. Upstairs, a replica of a Michelangelo ceiling fresco oversees marble fireplaces, tapestries, and a library. On the ground level, a long mahogany bar serves martinis and drinks of choice, while the downstairs club jams to techno, hip-hop, and retro sounds. ◈ *Map K5 • 770 5th Ave • (619) 338-9300 • Cover charge after 9:30pm Thu & after 8:30pm Fri–Sat*

Onyx Room
At this chic basement club, order the cocktail of the month and settle back in a vibrant lounge atmosphere. Upstairs is the Onyx's sister bar Thin, where the "engineered" drinks and atmosphere are the epitome of urban cool. ◈ *Map K5 • 852 5th Ave • (619) 235-6699 • Closed Mon, Wed, Sun • Cover charge Thu–Sat*

Sevilla
This restaurant-nightclub offers everything Latin. Tango and flamenco dinner shows spotlight

Entrance to the basement club at Onyx

the Spanish restaurant, while instructors teach salsa and samba downstairs. You can practice your moves to the live bands that perform afterwards. The basement becomes a Latin/ Euro dance club on Friday and Saturday nights. ◈ *Map J5 • 555 4th Ave • (619) 233-5979 • Cover charge*

Croce's Jazz Bar & Croce's Top Hat
Ingrid Croce opened Gaslamp's first club in tribute to her late husband, singer/songwriter Jim Croce, in 1985. The Jazz Bar features traditional, contemporary, and Latin live jazz, while the Top Hat features live R&B bands. However, tables are too close together and service can be indifferent. ◈ *Map K5 • 802 5th Ave • (619) 233-3660 • Cover charge*

El Dorado Cocktail Lounge
This classy boutique martini lounge with Wild West bordello-themed decor offers an amazing variety of entertainment, such as dance parties, DJs, live music, and art shows. The nightly events, top-notch service, and exceptional variety of drinks, such as specialty cocktails, draw in the crowds. ◈ *Map K4 • 1030 Broadway • (619) 237-0550 • Cover charge*

Prohibition
A small, intimate jazz bar with perfect martinis and a laid-back crowd that comes for the great music and friendly service. The bar has the feel of

Share your travel recommendations on traveldk.com

a secret club but welcomes all.
🚫 *Map K5 • 548 5th Ave • Closed Wed; reservations through website only • Cover charge*

Casbah

Underground alternative rock rules at this grungy club. Famous and future bands turn up the decibels every night. Past headliners have included Alanis Morissette, the Smashing Pumpkins, and Nirvana. 🚫 *Map H2 • 2501 Kettner Blvd • (619) 232-4355 • Cover charge*

Sign for Casbah

Ivy at Andaz

Located inside the Andaz Hotel, this nightclub is a glittering nightspot with sexy dancers from Thursday to Saturday. An open-air rooftop lounge combines DJ sets with private cabanas and panoramic views of the downtown skyline. 🚫 *Map J4 • 600 F St • (619) 814-2055 • Cover charge*

Humphrey's Backstage Live

Enjoy a variety of live music nightly at this waterfront lounge with an unbeatable view of the bay. Come early for a terrific happy hour. 🚫 *Map B5 • 2241 Shelter Island Dr • (619) 224-3577 • Cover charge for most bands*

National Comedy Theatre

With their unique brand of interactive and improv humor, the National Comedy Theatre's shows are popular and family-friendly. For each show, the audience choose a game and decide the winner. 🚫 *Map C4 • 3717 India St • (619) 295-4999 • Cover charge*

Top 10 Gay & Lesbian Venues

Spin
Three floors of bars and a dance club with Giant Fridays and Top 40 Saturdays. 🚫 *Map C4 • 2028 Hancock St • (619) 294-9590*

Bourbon Street
A piano bar with DJ and a dance floor at weekends and outlandish karaoke. 🚫 *Map D4 • 4612 Park Blvd • (619) 291-4043*

The Brass Rail
Dance to Latin or hip-hop at San Diego's oldest gay bar. 🚫 *Map C4 • 3796 5th Ave • (619) 298-2233*

Urban Mo's Bar & Grill
Rowdy, hetero-friendly drag club and grill. 🚫 *Map C4 • 308 University Ave • (619) 491-0400*

Pecs
Gay Harley-Davidson enthusiasts frequent this bar. 🚫 *Map C4 • 2046 University Ave • (619) 296-0889*

The Gossip Grill
Lesbian restaurant and bar with sensual atmosphere and great food. 🚫 *Map C4 • 1440 University Ave • (619) 260-8023*

Number One Fifth Ave
Video bar, pool table, and outdoor patio. 🚫 *Map C4 • 3845 5th Ave • (619) 299-1911*

Numbers
Pool tables, dartboards, giant video screens, and two dance floors. 🚫 *Map D4 • 3811 Park Blvd • (619) 294-7583*

Rich's
Glam go-go boys and girls dance to electronica. 🚫 *Map C4 • 1051 University Ave • (619) 295-2195*

Top of the Park
Piano bar at street level and Friday happy hour on the roof. 🚫 *Map C4 • 525 Spruce St • (619) 291-0999*

Left **Fishing** Right **Horse riding in Cuyamaca State Park**

🔟 Outdoor Activities

1 Cycling
With over 300 miles (483 km) of bikeways, San Diego is a very cycle-friendly city. iCommute's map details bike rides around the city and county and is available online. ◉ *iCommute: dial 511 and say "iCommute"; www.icommutesd.com • Bikes & Beyond: Map C6; 1201 1st St, Coronado; (619) 435-7180*

2 Sailing & Boating
Whether at Mission Bay or the Pacific Ocean, you're bound to see something that floats. You can rent almost any type of boat, complete with a crew, champagne, and hors d'oeuvres. ◉ *Seaforth Boat Rentals: Map B4 • 1641 Quivira Rd, Mission Bay • (888) 834-2628*

3 Sportfishing
Albacore, yellowfin, and dorado are just some of the fish in the offshore waters. Summer and fall are the best months, and half-, full-, and multiple-day trips are all available. A fishing license is not required to fish off the public piers. ◉ *Seaforth Sportfishing: Map B4 • 1717 Quivira Rd, Mission Bay • (619) 224-3383*

4 Swimming
Nothing beats an ocean dip, though the temperatures seldom exceed 70° F (21° C) even in the summer. Alternatively, you can find swimming pools at most hotels. The Plunge at the Wave House Athletic Club at Mission Beach is a great public pool. ◉ *The Plunge: Map A4 • 3115 Ocean Front Walk • (858) 228-9300 • Adm*

5 Surfing
San Diego's beaches are famous for surfing. The months with the strongest swells are in late summer and fall, ideally under offshore wind conditions. Designated surfing areas can be found at every beach. ◉ *San Diego Surfing Academy: (800) 447-7873*

6 Golfing
With San Diego's perfect climate and amazing views, over 90 public courses and resort hotels offer some of the best golfing in the country. Tee times may be hard to get, so reserve early. The San Diego Convention and Visitors Bureau (CVB) has a golf guide. ◉ *San Diego CVB: Map J6 • (619) 236-1212 • www.sandiego.org*

7 Rollerblading
Mission Bay and Pacific Beach are the best areas to enjoy the miles of pathway shared by skateboarders and joggers. Some areas of town specifically prohibit skating, so watch out for the signs. ◉ *Cheap Rentals: Map A4 • 3689 Mission Blvd • (858) 488-9070 • www.cheap-rentals.com*

Surfers at Swami's Beach, near Encinitas

Always ask a lifeguard about ocean conditions before plunging into the water.

Rollerblading

Hiking
Hiking is available in every environment imaginable. Los Peñasquitos Canyon Preserve and Mission Trails Regional Park *(see p46)* offer trails of varying difficulty through their canyons and valleys; the trails of Torrey Pines State Reserve and Tijuana River National Estuarine Research Reserve *(see p47)* pass near the ocean. The San Diego Natural History Museum *(see p18)* hosts guided nature tours.

Horseback Riding
Guided horseback rides are available on trails, through parks, and on the beach. The South Bay area offers the only beach where you can take an exhilarating ride on the sand and in the waves. There are also pony rides for children, hayrides, and romantic carriage rides. ◎ *Happy Trails: Map E3 • 2180 Monument Rd • (619) 662-2570 • www.happytrails-usa.com*

Diving
The best spots for diving off the coast are the giant kelp forests of Point Loma and the La Jolla Underwater Ecological Reserve. Common sealife includes lobsters and garibaldi – the official state marine fish. ◎ *San Diego Ocean Enterprises: Map B2 • 7710 Balboa Ave • (858) 565-6054*

Top 10 Spectator Sports

San Diego Chargers
Catch the American Football Conference team at Qualcomm Stadium. ◎ *Map D3 • (619) 280-2121*

San Diego Padres
Petco Park hosts the National League Padres' baseball team. ◎ *Map K6 • 100 Park Blvd • (619) 795-5000*

San Diego State University Aztecs
Take the San Diego Trolley out to Qualcomm Stadium. ◎ *Map E4*

San Diego Gulls Ice Hockey
The Gulls play in the ECHL Premier AA Hockey League. ◎ *Map B4 • 3500 Sports Arena Blvd • (619) 224-4625*

Del Mar Thoroughbred Club
Celebrities and horseracing fans head here. ◎ *Map D2 • 2260 Jimmy Durante Blvd, Del Mar • (858) 755-1141*

Hang gliding/ Paragliding
Hang gliders and paragliders take off from the ocean cliffs north of La Jolla *(see p62)*.

San Diego Polo Club
Attend polo matches on Sundays. ◎ *Map E2 • 14555 El Camino Real, Rancho Santa Fe • (858) 481-9217 • Adm*

Golf
Watch the annual golf tournaments at Torrey Pines and La Costa.

Mission Bay Park
Mission Bay hosts many boating events. ◎ *Map B3*

Bullfights
Check out the world's leading *toreros* at Plaza Monumental. ◎ *Map E3 • Playas de Tijuana, Tijuana • (664) 680-1808*

Colorful entrance to Viejas Casino

Offbeat San Diego

1 Paragliding at Torrey Pines
Soar off the spectacular cliffs of Torrey Pines *(see p33)*. In your first lesson, you'll receive basic instructions followed by 20–30 minutes of gliding with your instructor. If you'd like to watch for a while before making that exhilarating plunge, a viewing area and café sit on the cliff's edge. ◈ *Torrey Pines Gliderport: Map A1 • 2800 Torrey Pines Scenic Dr, La Jolla • (858) 452-9858*

2 Star of India Family Overnight Adventure
In August and September, the Maritime Museum offers a dockside Overnight Adventure for families aboard the *Star of India*. Guided by history experts, visitors learn what life was like on a sailing ship during the 1870s. They can raise a sail, hoist cargo, and sing sea shanties. Reservations are required *(see p42)*.

3 Rent a Harley Davidson
All of us are born to be wild, so put on your jeans and black leather jacket and rent a bike for a day. You won't be alone: droves of bikers take to the highway, especially on weekends. The backcountry of San Diego County is a prime area for powering a Fat Boy, Road King, or Dyna Wide Glide down the road. ◈ *Eagle Rider of San Diego: Map B4 • 4263 Taylor St • (619) 546-5066*

Harley-Davidson sign

Roar and Snore at the Zoo Safari Park

4 Roar & Snore at San Diego Zoo Safari Park
On weekends from May through November, sleep alongside wild animals just as you would in an African game park. Tents that hold up to four persons are provided. Programs include guided discovery hikes and animal encounters, an open-flame grilled dinner, campfire snacks, special late night programs, and a pancake breakfast before a gorgeous sunrise. Reservations are essential *(see p95)*.

5 Gambling at Indian Casinos
Feeling lucky? A dozen tribal casinos promise non-stop Las Vegas-style action and jackpots galore. Starting as a small bingo hall 20 years ago, Indian gaming is now a billion-dollar industry of resort hotels, concert venues, and golf courses. Today, San Diego County has the highest concentration of casinos in the state of California.

Thousands of slot machines, video poker, and gaming tables in immense, striking buildings will satisfy the gambler in you. ✎ *Viejas Casino: Map E2; 5000 Willows Rd, Alpine; (619) 445-5400 • Barona Resort & Casino: Map E2; 1932 Wildcat Canyon Rd, Lakeside; (619) 443-2300*

UFO Spotting in East County

Several San Diego groups take UFO (Unidentified Flying Object) sightings seriously. The best places to spot UFOs are in Borrego Springs and Ocotillo Wells. Given San Diego's strong military presence, that saucer in the sky might well be a secret government mission. ✎ *Map F1*

Hot-Air Ballooning

You can watch or take part in inflating a brilliantly colored balloon. Hop in the basket and begin to float over the valleys and hills with a glass of champagne in hand. Flights leave early in the morning or at sunset. Most hot-air balloon companies operate from Temecula where there are fewer housing developments to impede their landings. ✎ *California Dreamin': Map E1 • 33133 Vista del Monte Rd, Temecula • (800) 373-3359 • www. californiadreamin.com*

Biplane Flying

Two of you sit in the front cockpit of a beautifully restored 1920s biplane wearing helmet and goggles, and soar over beaches, lakes, golf courses, and houses, while the pilot flies behind. The *Beech Belle*, a restored World War II VIP biplane, is great for that special occasion. If you're looking for an extra thrill, the pilot will put you through aerobatic loops and rolls, or you can take the controls in

Hot-air ballooning

top dog air combat. ✎ *Barnstorming Adventures: Map E1 • Montgomery Field • (800) 759-5667 • www.barnstorming.com*

Diving at Wreck Alley

Just off Mission Beach is the final resting place for the *Yukon*, a decommissioned Canadian warship, the coastguard cutter *Ruby E*, and a barge, all deliberately sunk to create an artificial reef. A research tower here collapsed on its own, with its dangling wires and protrusions only adding to the otherworldly, ethereal atmosphere. Thousands of invertebrate marine life have taken up residence here. Charter boats will take you out. ✎ *Map A4*

Vintage Train Rides

Operated by the Railway Museum of San Diego, the Golden State Limited departs twice daily on the weekends from the historic Campo train depot, for a pleasant 12-mile (19-km) round trip to Miller Creek. Reserve a spot in the cab of the Diesel-electric locomotive and chat with the engineer and brakeman; you'll even have a chance to toot the horn. ✎ *Campo Depot: Map F3 • Hwy 94, Campo • (619) 478-9937 (weekends); (619) 465-7776 (weekdays)*

Silver Strand State Beach

🔟 Beaches

Silver Strand State Beach
Between Coronado and Imperial Beach, miles of the "Strand" attracts families with its wide expanses, gentle waves, fire rings, surf fishing, grunion runs (see p53) and, unique to San Diego beaches, clamming. The name Silver Strand comes from the tiny silver shells that dot the sand on the oceanside. Pedestrian tunnels lead to the beach on the bayside, where the water is warmer and calmer. ◎ Map E3

Ocean Beach
The laid-back atmosphere of Ocean Beach (see p85) attracts locals and some out-of-towners. Surfers usually go out around the pier, and swimmers farther down the beach. There tends to be a strong rip current at the beach, so don't swim out of sight from a lifeguard station. There are plenty of facilities, including showers, picnic tables, and volleyball courts. ◎ Map A4

Dog Beach
Leashes optional! Your dog can run loose to chase after balls, Frisbees, and other dogs with joyous abandon. The beach is open 24 hours, so you can even come here for a midnight swim. Posts with handy plastic bags help you pick up the aftermath. ◎ Map A4 • North end of Ocean Beach at San Diego River

Sailing at Mission Bay

Mission Beach
At this popular beach (see p97), sunburned, sandy bodies vie for space upon the sand, volleyballs and Frisbees fly overhead, and skateboarders and cyclists try to balance drinks and portable MP3 players as they careen down the boardwalk. If the beach scene gets overwhelming, Belmont Park (see p52) is just a block away. ◎ Map A4

Mission Bay Beaches
Protected from the waves of the Pacific Ocean, 27 miles (43 km) of shoreline, including 19 miles (30 km) of sandy beaches, coves, and inlets, offer idyllic picnic locations. On sunny days, the water is filled with sailboats, kayaks, waterskiers, windsurfers, and rowers. Bike paths wind for miles along the shoreline, and wide grassy areas and ocean breezes make flying kites ideal. ◎ Map B4

Playing volleyball at Ocean Beach

Pacific Beach

A great beach-going spirit fills the air as skateboarders, joggers, and cyclists cruise the promenade that runs parallel to the beach. People-watching opportunities are endless, since Pacific Beach has a reputation of being the place to hang out. Take a walk out to the Crystal Pier Hotel *(see p118)*, past the bungalows to watch surfers shooting the curl. ◈ *Map A3*

Crystal Pier Hotel at Pacific Beach

Windansea Beach

Legendary among surfers for its shorebreaks, this beach found literary fame as the setting for Tom Wolfe's *The Pumphouse Gang*. The beach gets a little wider south of the "Shack," a local landmark, but those with small children should still take care. ◈ *Map N3*

La Jolla Shores

A great family beach, but summertime gets crowded as sunbathers, Frisbee-throwers, and boogie-boarders spread out along a broad, sandy white strip lapped by gentle surf. Kellogg Park, which runs alongside part of the beach, is a good picnic area for those who forgot their towels. The La Jolla Underwater Ecological Reserve *(see p61)* is just offshore, so divers are usually out in the water. ◈ *Map Q1*

Black's Beach

This beach is notorious for its nude sunbathers. Access to the beach, which lies between Torrey Pines State Beach and La Jolla Shores, is either down an unstable 300-ft (91-m) cliff or via a 1-mile (1.6-km) walk along the beach from either the north or south during low tide. Surfers find the southern end of the beach ideal, as well as the hang-gliders who launch off from the cliffs above. ◈ *Map Q1*

Torrey Pines State Beach

Miles of sandy beaches and secret coves nestle beneath towering sandstone cliffs. During low tide, tide pools offer a glimpse into life under the sea. Torrey Pines is a San Diego favorite because of its lack of crowds, intimacy, and natural beauty. Parking is available at the Torrey Pines State Reserve *(see pp46–7)* or by the gliderport on top of the cliff. ◈ *Map A1*

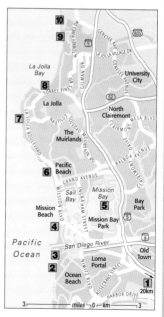

"Shorebreaks" are rough waves that break right on the shore.

Left **Cinco de Mayo celebration** Right **Christmas carols at Balboa Park**

Festivals

Mardi Gras

Be quick to grab the strings of beads thrown off the floats at the Masquerade Parade. The parade begins in the afternoon at Fifth Avenue, but music and revelry carries on until the early morning. The food booths serve up New Orleans-style Cajun food. ◉ *Gaslamp Quarter • Feb/Mar*

St. Patrick's Day Parade

A grand parade of marching bands, bagpipes, community organizations, horses, and school groups begins at Sixth and Juniper. Afterwards, an Irish festival takes place at Balboa Park with Irish dancers, lots to eat, green beer, and fun for the entire family. ◉ *Mar*

Cinco de Mayo

North of the Mexican border, commemorating the French defeat by Mexican troops is a serious business. Restaurants overflow, Old Town State Historic Park sponsors folkloric ballet performances and mariachi bands, and the Gaslamp Quarter hosts a musical street fair. ◉ *May*

Fourth of July Fireworks & Parades

Nearly every San Diego community has its own July 4th festivities, such as fireworks, surfing contests, parades, and street festivals. Since the ban of home fireworks, commercial fireworks shows are the way to go. The biggest show in the county is held over San Diego Harbor. ◉ *Jul*

Lesbian and Gay Parade and Festival

San Diego's gay community hits the streets in celebration of diversity. The parade begins at Fifth Avenue and Laurel in Hillcrest and moves to Balboa Park, where live bands, food booths, and a party atmosphere prevail. Outrageous costumes are the rule of the day. ◉ *End Jul*

St. Patrick's Day revelers

Halloween Festivals & Haunted Houses

Your worst nightmares may come true at the historic 1889 Haunted Hotel, which features ghouls, spooks, a clown asylum, and a haunted subway station. The Scream Zone at the Del Mar Fairgrounds has haunted hayrides pursued by zombies, and the infamous Chamber and Haunted Trails of Balboa Park will scare the wits out of you. ◉ *Gaslamp Quarter & Balboa Park • Oct • Adm*

Mother Goose Parade

Floats, equestrian units, clowns, marching bands, and drill teams make up only part of the 200 entries in the largest

Halloween scarecrow drinking on a porch

single-day event in San Diego County, attended by about 400,000 people annually. A tradition since 1947, the parade changes its theme every year but always revolves around a celebration of children. ◈ *El Cajon • Sun before Thanksgiving*

Christmas on the Prado
Balboa Park launches the Christmas season by opening its doors to the community. Museums are free after 5pm, carolers sing, and special food booths are set up. The park is closed to traffic, but shuttles reach the outer parking lots. Dress warmly and expect a crowd of over 50,000 people. ◈ *Balboa Park • First Fri & Sat of Dec*

Las Posadas
This is a traditional re-enactment of Mary and Joseph seeking shelter for the Christ child. A candlelight procession begins in Heritage Park, passing by historic homes and businesses that have food set out, and finishing at the plaza in Old Town State Historic Park. ◈ *Mid-Dec*

Boat Parades of Lights
Yachts and sailboats vie for the title of best decorated in Mission Bay and the San Diego Harbor. The best viewing areas for the Mission Bay parade are at Crown Point and Fiesta Island; for the San Diego Harbor Parade, head to the Embarcadero. ◈ *Dec*

Top 10 Fairs & Gatherings

1 Ocean Beach Kite Festival
A kite competition with prizes and demonstrations on the beach. ◈ *Ocean Beach • Mar*

2 Avocado Festival
Special tours, 50 food booths, and awards for best dishes attract huge crowds. ◈ *Fallbrook • Apr*

3 San Diego County Fair
Animals, rides, food, and music. ◈ *Del Mar • Jun • Adm*

4 A Taste of Gaslamp
A self-guided tour passes by restaurants displaying their kitchen samplings. ◈ *Gaslamp Quarter • Jun • Adm*

5 Mainly Mozart Festival
Concerts at San Diego and Tijuana feature works by the wunderkind and his contemporaries. ◈ *Apr–Jun • Adm*

6 US Open Sand Castle Competition
Competitors build the most complex and imaginative sand castles. ◈ *Imperial Beach • Aug*

7 Summerfest
Classical music and modern compositions in La Jolla, with artists and ensembles from around the world. ◈ *Aug*

8 Julian Fall Apple Harvest
Music, apple cider, and apple pies in a charming mountain town. ◈ *Mid-Sep–mid-Oct*

9 Cabrillo Festival
Soldiers re-enact the Cabrillo landing, and performers showcase Native American, Aztec, and Mayan dances. ◈ *Cabrillo National Monument • End Sep • Adm*

10 Fleet Week
Navy ship tours and air and sea parades honor the military. ◈ *Sep/Oct*

AROUND TOWN

SAN DIEGO'S TOP 10

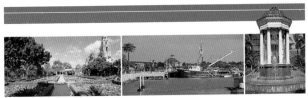

Left **Balboa Park** Center **Tuna Harbor, Embarcadero** Right **Fountain at Horton Plaza Park**

Downtown San Diego

SCARCELY A GENERATION AGO, *one drove through downtown San Diego with the windows rolled up, past derelict tattoo parlors, seedy tenements, and sleazy porn palaces. With vision and dedication, downtown has been transformed into a first-class destination for visitors and a trendy address for residents. Neighborhoods have blossomed with excellent restaurants, art galleries, and festivals; performing arts centers, museums, and a sports stadium attract visitors by the thousands. The atmosphere is strictly Southern*

Apes at San Diego Zoo

Californian: a blend of urban energy and laid-back priorities. Nowadays, drivers fight for cherished parking spaces and casual strolling is the preferred means of transport. From the edge of the Embarcadero, graced with 19th-century sailing ships, to the beautifully restored Victorian and Italianate buildings of the Gaslamp Quarter, a district straight out of the Wild West and home to trattorias, Irish pubs, and a pulsating nightlife, downtown is a great place to have fun in.

🔟 Sights

1. Gaslamp Quarter
2. Embarcadero
3. Balboa Park & San Diego Zoo
4. Westfield Horton Plaza
5. East Village
6. Little Italy
7. Asian Pacific Historic District
8. Museum of Contemporary Art
9. Martin Luther King Promenade
10. Marston House

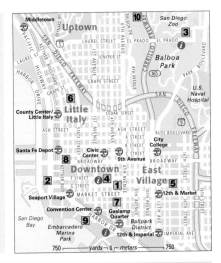

Previous pages: **Colorful house in Hillcrest**

Gaslamp Quarter

In the mid-19th century, the Gaslamp Quarter was the heart of a new city, but within 50 years it had fallen prey to gambling halls, opium dens, and houses of prostitution, and within another 50 years, it had become a broken-down slum. Now the Gaslamp Quarter sparkles as it looks to a brilliant future. During the day, the gloriously restored historic buildings, each an architectural highlight, attract history buffs and shoppers. By night, crowds line up to dine in fashionable restaurants, listen to music, or sip the latest martini concoction (see pp8–9).

Buildings in the Gaslamp Quarter

Embarcadero

For those arriving by ship or train, the Embarcadero is San Diego's front door. Passengers disembark from gleaming white cruise ships tied up at B Street Pier or pass through a 1915 train depot, eager to enjoy the city's attractions. But unlike most cities, the Embarcadero is an attraction in itself. Pedestrian-friendly walkways pass by historic sailing ships, museums, shopping centers, and parks. Serious and quirky public art works and a splendid harbor filled with maritime life define this lively district (see pp10–11).

Balboa Park & San Diego Zoo

Home to the world-famous San Diego Zoo, 15 unique museums, theaters, countless recreational opportunities, and exquisite landscaping, Balboa Park creates an indelible impression. No matter the time of year, vibrant flowers bloom in profusion and pepper tree groves and grassy expanses provide idyllic spots for picnicking. Allow a minimum of a few days to soak in the park's attractions (see pp14–19).

White floss silk tree flower at the Zoo

Westfield Horton Plaza

When it opened in 1985, developers kept their fingers crossed that this unique shopping center would draw visitors to a declining area and help spearhead a downtown revival. It was an immediate hit – people loved the Plaza's inward-facing design, tiered shopping levels, and the 43 unusual colors of paint on its walls. Covering several city blocks, the plaza features more than 130 shops, movie theaters, and stage productions at the Lyceum Theatre (see p50). Adjacent to Westfield Horton Plaza is the Balboa Theatre (see p9). Built as a cinema in 1924, it now offers live performances.

Cyclists along the Embarcadero

East Village
5 Formerly a Victorian village that fell into neglect but survived as a warehouse district and artist colony, this redeveloped area is now very fashionable. Petco Park, the 2004 state-of-the-art baseball stadium and home to the San Diego Padres *(see p61)*, is the neighborhood's major focal point. Check out the 1909 Western Metal Supply building: architects incorporated the vintage building into the stadium's structure. A Children's Museum of San Diego, shops, restaurants, and residential high-rises have opened here, with a new library due to open in 2013. ◈ *Map L5*

Little Italy
6 This revitalized downtown neighborhood is one of San Diego's oldest. Genoese fishing families were the first Italians to settle along the waterfront in the 1860s. Along with Portuguese immigrants, they founded San Diego's prosperous tuna industry. Little Italy, sometimes also known as Middletown, has now become a fashionable address. While retaining its Bohemian character, Italian restaurants, art galleries, antique and design stores, and hip cafés distinguish its streets. ◈ *Map J3*

Little Italy

Asian Pacific Historic District
7 An eight-block area that overlaps part of the Gaslamp Quarter designates the former center of San Diego's Asian community. The Chinese came to San Diego following the California Gold Rush and took up fishing and construction work; others ran opium dens and gambling halls. Filipino and Japanese communities soon followed. This is the home of Chinese New Year celebrations, a farmers' market, and an Asian bazaar. Join a walking tour at the Chinese Historical Museum *(see p42)*, and look out for the Asian architectural flourishes on the buildings you pass by. ◈ *Map J5*

Museum of Contemporary Art
8 This two-building downtown location of the museum in La Jolla *(see p32)*, presents rotating exhibits from emerging and established contemporary artists, as well as selected pieces from the museum's permanent collection. Marking the entrance is the 18-ft (5.4-m) *Hammering Man at 3,110,527*, a steel and aluminum sculpture by Jonathan Borofsky. The museum also hosts lectures, workshops, and family activities, including the popular free opening on the third Thursday evening of each month, when there is a themed gallery tour.

The Founding of Modern San Diego

When entrepreneur Alonzo Horton arrived in a burgeoning San Diego in 1867, he believed that a new city could prosper in this location. He bought 960 acres and sold and even gave away lots to people. When you walk the Gaslamp Quarter, note the short blocks and lack of alleys, created due to the opinion that corner lots were worth more and alleys only accumulated trash.

⊗ *Map H4* • *1001 & 1100 Kettner Blvd*
• *(858) 454-3541* • *Open 11am–5pm
Thu–Tue (11am–7pm 3rd Thu each
month)* • *Docent-led tours 6pm 3rd Thu
each month (free), 2pm Sat, Sun* • *Adm*

9 Martin Luther King Promenade

Planner Max Schmidt used the idea of functional public art to create this 1/4-mile (0.4-km) promenade along Harbor Drive. Described as a "serape" of colors, textures, and water-works, the grassy promenade celebrates San Diego's multi-cultural heritage. Granite stones in the sidewalk bear quotes by civil-rights leader Dr. Martin Luther King. ⊗ *Map H5*

10 Marston House

This fine Arts and Crafts house, built in 1905, is now open to the public as a museum. The exterior combines elements of Victorian and English Tudor styles, while the interior offers expansive hallways and intimate living spaces. Adorned with Mission-style furnishings, there are fine pottery, paintings, and textiles by craftsman artisans. The museum is operated by the San Diego Historical Society.
⊗ *Map K1* • *3525 7th Ave* • *(619) 298-3142* • *Open for docent-led tours only: half-hourly tours start at 10am; last tour begins at 4:30pm* • *Adm*

A Day Walking Around Downtown

Morning

Start at the **Santa Fe Depot**. Walk right on Broadway, cross the RR tracks, and walk two blocks to Harbor Drive. Turn right and head to the **Maritime Museum of San Diego** *(see p42)*. Check out the exhibits and climb aboard the *Star of India*. Walk back down Harbor Drive to the ticket booth for harbor tours. A narrated harbor cruise brings you close to the naval facilities. Next, spend an hour or so aboard the **USS *Midway*** at the **USS Midway Museum** *(see pp12–13)*. Finally, it's time for lunch at **The Fish Market** *(see p54)*.

Afternoon

Continue down Harbor Drive to **Seaport Village** *(see p11)* and stay on the sidewalk until you reach a crossing. Turn left; walk up the street past the **Manchester Grand Hyatt Hotel**, across Harbor Drive and the trolley tracks. Walk onto the **Martin Luther King Promenade**, which stretches past beautiful downtown apartment revitalizations. At the Convention Center trolley stop, turn left, then left again on J St. On J and 3rd, stop by the **San Diego Chinese Historical Museum** *(see p42)*. Turn left on 3rd and right on Island; you'll pass the historic **Horton Grand Hotel**. At 4th, visit the **William Heath Davis House** *(see p8)*. One block farther is the heart of the **Gaslamp Quarter**. After walking around, treat yourself to a sundae at **Ghirardelli Soda Fountain** at 631 5th Street.

Left **Exterior of Bubbles Boutique** Right **Exterior of San Diego Harley Davidson**

Shopping

Hatworks
Knowledgeable staff will help you find the perfect hat for any occasion from an exceptional selection of hats from around the world in many styles and sizes. ⊗ *Map K5* • *433 E St* • *(619) 234-0457*

San Diego Harley Davidson
At this official boutique, the Harley Davidson logo is emblazoned on everything, including T-shirts, shot glasses, key chains, and kids' clothes. ⊗ *Map H5* • *Seaport Village* • *(619) 234-5780*

Hot DOGity Do's
This place specializes in fancy grooming for cats and dogs, and sells lots of high-end treats, leashes, collars, toys, and food for pets. ⊗ *Map J5* • *G St between 7th and 8th Ave* • *(619) 237-9073*

Urban Outfitters
This one-stop clothing shop for the young and trendy never lags behind the latest styles. Their original home accessories with an urban edge are true conversation pieces. ⊗ *Map K5* • *665 5th Ave* • *(619) 231-0102*

Pannikin Coffee and Tea
This magical place is filled with treasures from all over the world, such as festive Rajasthani umbrellas, beaded chairs from Nigeria, Mexican sugar skull molds, countless tea sets, and coffee, tea, and spices. ⊗ *Map K5* • *675 G St* • *(619) 239-7891*

Chuck Jones Gallery
Fine animation and entertainment art by famous artist Chuck Jones and other well-known animators, such as Dr. Seuss, are for sale in this gallery setting. ⊗ *Map K5* • *232 5th Ave* • *(619) 294-9880*

Bubbles Boutique
Come here for trendy and fun casualwear, luxurious pajamas, hand-crafted bath products, and a great selection of one-of-a-kind gifts and accessories. ⊗ *Map K5* • *226 5th Ave* • *(619) 236-9003*

The Cuban Cigar Factory
Cigar makers roll tobacco from Central America and the Dominican Republic in San Diego's original cigar factory. Aficionados can select from a variety of cigars and admire the humidors on display. ⊗ *Map K5* • *551 5th Ave* • *(619) 238-2496*

Architectural Salvage of San Diego
Head here for Victorian cutglass doorknobs and handles, clawfoot bathtubs, leaded glass, and vintage doors. ⊗ *Map H3* • *2401 Kettner Blvd* • *(619) 696-1313*

Carol Gardyne
Carol creates original and limited edition hand-painted si scarves, women's clothing, a wall hangings that depict na with abstract shapes in bril or subtle hues. ⊗ *Map H2* • Columbia St • *(619) 233-8066*

Store at San Diego Museum of Man

TOP 10 Museum Shops

1 Mingei International Museum

This store is filled with ethnic clothes, Chinese brushes, Russian dolls, Indian chiming bells, and a good selection of *alebrijes* (see p18).

2 San Diego Museum of Art

Merchandise reflects special exhibits. Wonderful art books, stationery, jewelry, purses, flower pressing kits, and Tibetan chests are for sale. The children's section offers educational toys, games, and gifts (see p18).

3 San Diego Museum of Man

Crafts from around Latin America include carved Peruvian gourds, textiles, Mexican folk art, and three-legged Chilean good luck pigs. There is also a wide assortment of Native American crafts such as silver jewelry (see p18).

4 Museum of Contemporary Art

If you're looking for art gifts with a contemporary edge, you might find them among the select merchandise that relates to the museum's special exhibitions. Always on display are the latest art books and handcrafted jewelry (see pp72–3).

5 Reuben H. Fleet Science Center

Science toys, videos, puzzles, and hands-on games will attract the kids – and you (see p52).

6 Maritime Museum of San Diego

Gratify your nautical gift needs through a variety of model ships, T-shirts, posters, and prints inscribed with an image of the *Star of India* (see p42).

7 San Diego Art Institute Shop

Juried art shows showcase the work of local artists, whose works often go on sale after being exhibited. This small shop features glass sculptures, porcelain *objets d'art*, hand-painted cushions, and jewelry.
⊗ Map L1 • House of Charm, Balboa Park

8 San Diego Chinese Historical Museum

Chinese calligraphy sets, snuff bottles, tea sets, and chops – a type of carved stamp traditionally used to sign one's name – are on sale here (see p42).

9 San Diego History Center

If you're interested in the history of San Diego, including haunted locations and biographies of various characters, this museum offers one of the best collections of local history books (see p18).

10 San Diego Zoo Shops

Several gift shops at the zoo sell items from around the world, including jewelry, African art, clothing, books, and music. Stuffed toys, such as pandas, and gourmet foods are popular buys (see p14 and pp16–17).

Alebrijes are a type of Mexican folk art from Oaxaca that feature whimsical, painted wooden animals and figurines.

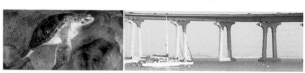

Left **East Pacific green sea turtle** Right **Coronado Bridge**

🔟 Cruising the Bay

1 Museum Vessels of the Embarcadero
The sailing ship *Star of India* dates back to 1863; *Berkeley* used to carry passengers in the Bay Area; and the USS *Midway* features in the USS Midway Museum *(see pp10–13)*.

2 SPAWAR
The Navy marine mammal facility trains bottlenose dolphins, with their biological sonar, to locate sea mines. ◈ *Map D6*

3 Cabrillo National Monument
Dedicated to the European discovery of San Diego and Alta California, this monument draws over one million people a year. The statue of Cabrillo is a replica of an original that could not withstand the wind and salt air *(see p26)*.

4 Naval Air Station North Island
Several aircraft carriers tie up here. You can often see high-tech aircraft, submarines, and destroyers take off and land *(see p25)*.

5 Local Marine Wildlife
Seals and sea lions are typical residents of the bay. The endangered East Pacific green sea turtle and the California least tern have protected foraging habitats.

6 Coronado Bridge
This distinctive bridge links Coronado to San Diego. Its gradual incline and curve allows cars to maintain speed, and the bridge sits high enough to allow aircraft carriers to pass beneath at high tide *(see p24)*.

7 Naval Base San Diego
Composed of 13 piers, this base provides shore support and living quarters for more than 50 naval ships of the Pacific Fleet, and is one of only two major fleet support installations in the country. ◈ *Map D6*

8 NASSCO Shipyard
The National Steel and Ship-building Company designs and builds US Navy auxiliary ships, commercial tankers, and container ships. It is one of the largest shipyards in the US. ◈ *Map D6*

9 Naval Amphibious Base
Home to the Navy SEALS and the Navy Parachute Team, the facility has served as an amphibious training base since 1943. The base is responsible for training, maintenance, and crews of the ships of the Pacific Fleet *(see p25)*.

10 Cruise Ship Terminal
San Diego boasts the fastest-growing cruise ship port on the west coast, with 180 ships docking at the B Street Pier throughout the year. Cruises leave port for excursions to the Mexican Riviera, Hawaii, Canada, the Panama Canal, and the South Pacific. ◈ *Map G4*

These are all sights that are pointed out while on a harbor cruise; most cannot be visited.

Price Categories

Price categories include a three-course meal for one, half a bottle of wine, and all unavoidable extra charges including tax.

$	under $20
$$	$20–$40
$$$	$40–$55
$$$$	$55–$80
$$$$$	over $80

Sign at The Cheese Shop

🔟 Places to Eat

1 Oceanaire Seafood Room
The upscale creative menu here features fresh seafood from around the world. The oysters and crab cakes are legendary. ✪ *Map J5 • 400 J St • (619) 858-2277 • $$$*

2 Acqua Al 2 Restaurant
Regularly voted the best Italian restaurant in San Diego, diners come here for the authentic Tuscan cuisine served in a cozy, intimate setting. ✪ *Map J5 • 322 5th Ave • (619) 230-0382 • $$$*

3 The Grant Grill
Sporting a club-like ambience with modern touches, The Grant Grill offers contemporary California cuisine. Try the crab cake with relish and tangerine sauce. ✪ *Map J4 • US Grant Hotel, 326 Broadway • (619) 744-2077 • $$$$*

4 Top of the Market
The chichi sister of the Fish Market *(see p54)*. Come here for a window seat, a quieter atmosphere, and seafood prepared with panache. ✪ *Map G5 • 750 N. Harbor Dr • (619) 232-3474 • $$$$$*

5 Athens Market Taverna
Expect a sensational presentation of classic Greek dishes. The menu relies heavily on fish and meat. ✪ *Map J5 • 109 W. F St • (619) 234-1955 • Closed Sun • $$$*

6 Red Pearl Kitchen
Chinese and East Asian food is served with flair in this trendy Gaslamp Quarter restaurant. Deep-red walls and contemporary decor add glamour. ✪ *Map J5 • 440 J St • (619) 231-1100 • $$$*

7 Karl Strauss' Brewing Company
Try the outstanding burgers, blackened salmon, or baby back ribs. A range of house brews celebrate the local spirit. ✪ *Map H4 • 1157 Columbia St • (619) 234-2739 • $$*

8 Osteria Panevino
Enjoy creative, affordable Italian cuisine in this casual Tuscan farmhouse-style setting. ✪ *Map J5 • 722 5th Ave • (619) 595-7959 • $$*

9 The Cheese Shop
Locals line up here for monster-sized custom sandwiches. Roast pork loin and roast beef are specialties, along with a wide selection of cheese. ✪ *Map J5 • 311 Island Ave • (619) 232-2303 • $*

10 St. Tropez Bakery & Bistro
Feast on stuffed croissants, crêpes, and well-prepared salads. Save room for utterly delicious pastries. A little wine bar is attached. ✪ *Map H4 • 600 W. Broadway/ 130 America Plaza • (619) 234-2560 • $*

Around Town – Downtown San Diego

Unless otherwise stated, all restaurants are open daily, accept credit cards, serve vegetarian meals, and provide disabled access.

Left & Center **Belltower & Mission Basilica San Diego de Alcalá** Right **Gay poster in Hillcrest**

Old Town, Uptown, & Mission Valley

THIS LONG STRETCH *follows the San Diego River from the Mission San Diego de Alcalá to Old Town. Over 200 years ago, Kumeyaay Indians lived in tribal groups within small settlements in the valley. Unknown to them, strangers from the other side of the earth would change their lives forever.*

Sights

1 Old Town State Historic Park

2 Mission Basilica San Diego de Alcalá

3 Hillcrest

4 Junípero Serra Museum

5 Heritage Park

6 University of San Diego

7 Whaley House

8 Presidio Park

9 Mormon Battalion Memorial Visitor's Center

10 Mission Hills

Spanish soldiers and Franciscan padres would have their time of glory here, as well as San Diego's pioneer families. Today, the valley itself holds little interest beyond masses of chain motels and shopping centers intersected by a freeway; however, on the bluffs above, you'll find eclectic neighborhoods overflowing with charm, brilliant architecture, and chic restaurants. Tolerance and diversity creates a progressive, Bohemian air, while rising real estate prices have turned simple bungalow homes into showpieces. And San Diego's birthplace is always close by.

Statuette, Mission Basilica San Diego de Alcalá

Old Town Plaza, State Historic Park

1 Old Town State Historic Park

San Diego's first commercial settlement has been either preserved or re-created in this pedestrian-only park. Although much of the town was destroyed in a fire in 1872, prompting the development of a new town center closer to the water, several of the original structures still remain. You can wander into any of Old Town's houses and find museums or concession shops inside, or enjoy one of the park's many Mexican restaurants *(see pp22–3)*.

2 Mission Basilica San Diego de Alcalá

A peaceful enclave among the non-descript strip malls of Mission Valley, the mission's original spirit still lingers in the church and its lovely gardens. The first of California's 21 missions was moved to this permanent site a few years after its founding. Over the years, the structure was re-built to suit the needs of the time, transforming it from a simple mission to a fortress with 5- to 7-ft (1.5- to 2-m) thick adobe brick walls. Its famous façade and bell tower have inspired architects to copy the "Mission Style" throughout San Diego *(see pp28–9)*.

3 Hillcrest

Considered San Diego's first suburb in the 1920s, Hillcrest slowly developed into a residential area, offering a quiet alternative to the bustle of downtown. A trolley stop opened the neighborhood up to thriving businesses, restaurants, and theaters; in the 1940s merchants proudly erected a sign that spanned University Boulevard, proclaiming "Hillcrest" to the world. But fortunes changed, neglect followed, and the sign came down. In the 1970s, the gay and lesbian community took up the revitalization challenge and transformed the community into a hip destination with great restaurants, nightlife, and avant-garde shops. And the sign is back – in neon. ◎ *Map C4*

4 Junípero Serra Museum

Constructed in 1929 to a design by architect William Templeton Johnson, the museum building is in keeping with the city's Spanish-Colonial heritage. Its white stucco arches, narrow passages, red-tile roof, and stately tower pay tribute to the first mission, which stood near this site. The San Diego Historical Society oversees the museum, which is dedicated to the city's earliest days. Artifacts from on-going archeological excavations at the presidio, ceramics made by Kumeyaay Indians, clothing, furniture, and a cannon help illustrate the meager life people led. Climb the tower to compare today's view with that of 1929. ◎ *Map P4 • 2727 Presidio Dr • (619) 232-6203 • Open 10am–5pm Sat–Sun • Adm • www.sandiegohistory.org*

Junípero Serra Museum

Heritage Park

Downtown's rapid expansion after World War II almost destroyed several Victorian heritage houses and San Diego's first synagogue. The Save Our Heritage Organization rescued and moved these architectural treasures to this specially created park. Of notable interest is the Sherman Gilbert House, once home to art and music patrons Bess and Gertrude Gilbert, who hosted luminaries such as Artur Rubinstein, Anna Pavlova, and the Trapp Family Singers. Bronze plaques describe the houses' former lives.
⊗ *Map P5 • 2454 Heritage Park Row
• (619) 819-6009 • Open 9am–5pm daily*

University of San Diego

Grand Spanish Renaissance buildings distinguish this independent Catholic university, its design inspired by the university in the Spanish town of Alcalá de Henares. Of exceptional note is the Founders Chapel with its white marble altar, gold-leaf decoration, 14 stained-glass nave windows, and marble floor. The campus is known for the Joan B. Kroc School of Peace Studies and its programs in law, education, nursing, and engineering. ⊗ *Map C4 • 5998 Alcalá Park • (619) 260-4600*

Plaque at Presidio Park

University of San Diego

Apolinaria Lorenzana

In 1800, Apolinaria Lorenzana and 20 orphans arrived from Mexico to be distributed to respectable presidio families. She taught herself to write by copying every written thing she found. She spent her life caring for the mission padres, teaching children and women church doctrine, and tending the sick. Nicknamed La Beata, she was one of the few women to receive a land grant.

Whaley House

California's first two-story brick structure also served as San Diego's first courthouse, county seat, and home to Thomas Whaley, who built this house in 1856 over a graveyard and site of a former gallows. Considered one of the most haunted in America, the US Commerce Department declared the house officially haunted in the 1960s. ⊗ *Map P5 • 2482 San Diego Ave • (619) 297-7511 • Open 10am–5pm Sun–Tue, 10am–9:30pm Thu–Sat; late May–early Sep: 10am–9:30pm daily • Adm*

Presidio Park

Kumeyaay Indians once used this hillside for sacred ceremonies. Site of the original Spanish presidio and mission settlement, a lovely park is all that's left of San Diego's beginnings. The park contains the Junípero Serra Museum *(see p79)* and the remaining earthen walls of Fort Stockton, a fortress that changed hands several times during the Mexican-American War, commemorated by bronze monuments, a flagpole, and a cannon. The 28-ft (8.5-m) Serra Cross, constructed from mission tiles, honors Father Junípero Serra *(see p29)*. ⊗ *Map P5*

Mormon Battalion Memorial Visitor's Center

Mormon Battalion Memorial Visitor's Center

In July 1846, 500 men, 32 women, and 51 children set out from Council Bluffs, Iowa, on what would be considered one of the longest military marches in history. Six months and 2,000 miles (3,218 km) later, they arrived in San Diego to offer support to the American military garrison during the Mexican-American War. At the Visitor's Center, a volunteer from the Church of Latter-Day Saints will discuss the historic march and Mormon contributions to San Diego and California. ⊗ Map P5
• 2510 Juan St • (619) 298-3317
• Open 9am–9pm daily

Mission Hills

One of San Diego's most charming and romantic neighborhoods is tucked in the hills overlooking Old Town and San Diego Bay. Tree-lined streets run past architectural jewels built in Craftsman, Mission Revival, Italian Renaissance, and Victorian style. Dating from the early 20th century, homes had to cost at least $3,500, and could not keep any male farm animals. Commercial development was restricted, and only those of Caucasian descent could hold property. Still here is Kate Sessions' 1910 nursery (see p19). ⊗ Map Q5 • Mission Hills Nursery: 1525 Fort Stockton Dr

A Walk Around Old Town, Heritage Park, & Presidio Park

Morning

🕐 Begin at the **Old Town Transit Center**. Cross the street and follow the path into **Old Town State Historic Park**. Just to the left is the **Interpretive Center**, where you can pick up a map. Walk along the right side of the Plaza and peek into the Bailey & McGuire Pottery Shop. Follow the signs to the **Casa de Machado-Stewart** and the **Mason Street School** (see p23). Back at the Plaza, visit the **La Casa de Estudillo** (see p22) for the best insight into an upper-class home of early California. From the Plaza's southwest corner, continue out of the State Park. Walk along San Diego Avenue, where you'll find souvenir shops, galleries, and restaurants. Try the **Old Town Mexican Café** (see p83) for lunch.

Afternoon

Cross the street at Conde and backtrack up San Diego Avenue to visit the haunted **Whaley House**. Turn right on Harney Street and walk uphill to **Heritage Park**. Backtrack one block to the **Mormon Battalion Visitor's Center**. Turn right on Juan Street and walk to Mason. You'll see a sign indicating "The Old Presidio Historic Trail." Turn right on Mason, follow the golf course to Jackson, and look for the footpath across the street. You'll parallel Jackson to the left and wind uphill to **Presidio Park**. Across the grass are the ruins of the original presidio, the **Serra Cross**, and the **Junípero Serra Museum**.

Left **Original Paw Pleasers** Right **Bazaar del Mundo**

Shopping

Bazaar del Mundo
Lining a lushly landscaped plaza decorated in brilliant colors, quality shops offer Mexican tableware, folk art, Guatemalan textiles, and books. 🖎 *Map N5 • 4133 Taylor St • (619) 296-3161*

Circa a.d.
Discover decorating ideas among the exotic home accents, antiques, and teak furniture, mostly from China and Southeast Asia. Planters fill the outside. 🖎 *Map N4 • 5355 Grant St • (619) 293-3328*

Babette Schwartz
Come here to find a wacky item to make you the life of the party. The eclectic selection of trendy, funny gifts changes frequently. 🖎 *Map C4 • 421 University Ave • (619) 220-7048*

Four Winds Trading Company
This Old Town store specializes in authentic Indian pottery, weavings, jewelry, dreamcatchers, and paintings of Native American themes. 🖎 *Map P5 • 2448-B San Diego Ave • (619) 692-0466*

Twirl Inc
This popular boutique with friendly staff offers affordable, unique women's fashion. 🖎 *Map C4 • 3840 5th Ave • (619) 291-0933*

Village Hat Shop
If you want to keep the sun off your head, this is the right place: find Panama hats, straw and felt hats, and other imaginative creations on display. 🖎 *Map C4 • 3821 4th Ave • (619) 683-5533*

Original Paw Pleasers
If you feel guilty about leaving your dog or cat at home, bribe him or her with a fresh baked treat or liver-flavored ice-cream from this pet bakery. 🖎 *Map D4 • 2818 University Ave • (619) 293-7297*

Old Town Market
This festive market offers entertainment and local artisans. The shops sell colorful Mexican goods, including Day of the Dead folk art, textiles, and Talavera ceramics. There are also boutiques that stock Southwestern silver jewelry and gifts. 🖎 *Map N5 • 4010 Twiggs St • (619) 260-1078*

Whole Foods
With an emphasis on fresh organic food, you'll find flavorful produce, a great assortment of imported goods, and a deli that specializes in healthy takeout. 🖎 *Map C4 • 711 University Ave • (619) 294-2800*

Adams Avenue & Park Boulevard Antique Row
Still untouched by San Diego's urban renewal boom, antique stores, second-hand book and record shops, and retro-clothing boutiques are sprinkled along these streets in east Hillcrest and Normal Heights. 🖎 *Adams Ave: Map D4 • Park Blvd: Map D4*

Price Categories

Price categories include a three-course meal for one, half a bottle of wine, and all unavoidable extra charges including tax.	**$** under $20
	$$ $20–$40
	$$$ $40–$55
	$$$$ $55–$80
	$$$$$ over $80

Yellow Corvette in the Corvette Diner

🔟 Places to Eat

1 Jack and Guilio's Italian Restaurant
Classics like Caprese salad, scampi, and tiramisu are served in a romantic and intimate space, which provides a welcome respite from the crowds in Old Town. ◈ Map P5 • 2391 San Diego Ave • (619) 294-2074 • $$$

2 Corvette Diner
Cruise back to the 1950s in this diner decorated with hub-caps, vintage gas station signs, and a yellow Corvette. ◈ Map C4 • 2965 Historic Decatur Rd • (619) 542-1476 • $

3 Wellington Steak and Martini Lounge
Classy and intimate, this modern restaurant serves great steaks and exceptional martinis. ◈ Map C4 • 741 W. Washington St • (619) 295-6001 $$$

4 El Agave Tequileria
Utter culinary magic awaits within one of the first tequilarias in San Diego. Classic Mexican food with French touches make eating here an event (see p54).

5 25 Forty Bistro & Bakehouse
This bistro serves a mix of Italian and French dishes made with fresh produce. ◈ Map N5 • 2540 Congress St • (619) 294-2540 • Closed Tue • $$

6 Blue Water Seafood Market & Grill
A fabulous selection of fresh seafood is on offer at this friendly down-home seafood market. Try the fish tacos, seafood cocktails, or chowders. ◈ Map C4 • 3667 India St • (619) 497-0914 • $$

7 Old Town Mexican Café & Cantina
Watch the famous "Tortilla Ladies of Old Town." People line up to try the café's grilled pork carnitas and chilaquiles, a delicious tortilla strip casserole. ◈ Map P5 • 2489 San Diego Ave • (619) 297-4330 • $$

8 Lefty's Chicago Pizzeria
Chicago-style pizza, hot dogs, fries, and beef sandwiches are the specialties at this family-owned eatery. ◈ Map D4 • 3448 30th St • (619) 295-1720 • Closed Mon • $$

9 Bread & Cie
Breads such as anise and black-olive loaf are baked and made into unusual sandwiches here. ◈ Map C4 • 350 University Ave • (619) 683-9322 • No credit cards • $

10 Chicken Pie Shop
Seniors and budget-eaters love the hearty food here. Mashed potatoes and gravy accompany tasty chicken pies. ◈ Map D4 • 2633 El Cajon, North Park • (619) 295-0156 • No credit cards • $

Unless otherwise stated, all restaurants are open daily, accept credit cards, serve vegetarian meals, and provide disabled access.

83

Left **Cabrillo National Monument** Center **Ocean Beach** Right **San Diego International Airport**

Southern San Diego

SOUTH OF SAN DIEGO *to the Mexican border, cultures blend irrevocably. Many Mexican citizens live, work in, and send their children to school in communities such as Chula Vista and National City. Likewise, many Americans live in the beach towns south of Tijuana, taking advantage of cheaper housing and medical care. And people flood both ways across the border to shop, to be entertained, and to pursue a livelihood. Vast stretches of empty beaches are protected nature preserves where one can hike and discover abundant wildlife. Beach towns devote themselves to the surf culture, while exclusive Coronado boasts one of the most prized zip codes in the country.*

Left **Coronado Bridge** Right **Old Point Loma Lighthouse**

🔟 Sights

1. Coronado
2. Point Loma
3. Tijuana
4. Ocean Beach
5. San Diego International Airport
6. Shelter Island
7. Harbor Island
8. Marine Corps Recruit Depot
9. Border Field State Park
10. Chula Vista Nature Center

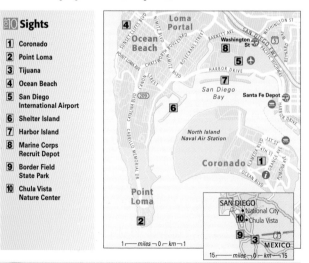

Coronado

In the 1880s, two wealthy businessmen, Elisha Babcock, Jr. and Hampton Story, purchased Coronado and set out to build a town. They sold lots, laid streets, and constructed the landmark Hotel del Coronado *(see p115)*. John D. Spreckels *(see p39)* soon bought them out and turned Coronado into a haven for old-money gentry. The military permanently took over much of the peninsula during World War I. The old mansions, resorts, and military base exist harmoniously and give Coronado its unique identity *(see pp24–5)*.

Point Loma

Over one million people a year visit the Cabrillo National Monument at Point Loma. The views are simply mesmerizing, and the peninsula ends at the meeting point of the Pacific Ocean and San Diego Bay. Half the peninsula is occupied by the military, which has prevented over-development. Spend time at Sunset Cliffs Park to experience the wind and sea and perhaps spot a whale *(see pp26–7)*.

Tijuana

During the days of Prohibition, Tijuana used to be the destination of choice for the Hollywood elite and their followers, and for alcohol and gambling. The palatial, Moorish-designed Agua Caliente Casino & Spa *(see p35)* was so popular that it boasted its own landing airstrip for the private planes of the wealthy. Fortunes fell when Mexico declared casino gambling illegal in 1935. US Navy servicemen soon added to Tijuana's reputation at the bars on Avenida Revolución, but nowadays, the city has cleaned up its image considerably. Take the time and you'll find culture and great food in Mexico's fourth largest city *(see pp34–5)*.

Ocean Beach

Unconventional and laid back, OB, as it's locally known, still has a somewhat hippie-like feel from the 1970s. On Newport Avenue, its main thoroughfare, you can still find a few original head shops. But OB is mainly about the beach: on any day of the year, surfers are next to the pier waiting for the next swell; volleyball players are spiking balls over the net; and dogs and their owners are running freely on Dog Beach *(see p64)*.

San Diego International Airport

No matter where you are in San Diego, look up and you'll see a jet soaring dramatically past the downtown high-rises on its final approach to Lindbergh Field *(see p40)* as locals call the airport. One hundred years ago, this area was a muddy wasteland that proved to be an ideal spot for budding inventors and pilots to try out their latest machines. In 1927, Ryan Aviation *(see p39)* designed, produced, and tested on the beach the *Spirit of St. Louis*, the historic plane that Charles Lindbergh piloted solo across the Atlantic. ◈ Map C5

Street singers in Tijuana

85

Shelter Island Yacht Harbor in San Diego Bay

Shelter Island

Not really an island but a peninsula that juts out into San Diego Bay from Point Loma, the "island" is home to thousands of pleasure boats and a park that stretches along its length. In the 1950s, the city dredged millions of tons of sand and mud from the bay onto a sandbar to create land for marinas and hotels. A number of hotels still have hints of Polynesian themes, a popular style at the time. At the entrance to Shelter Island is the San Diego Yacht Club, the three-time host of the prestigious America's Cup sailing race. ⊗ Map B5

Harbor Island

Created from 3.5 million tons of mud scooped from the bottom of San Diego Bay, this recreational island is another peninsula that extends into the bay south from the airport. Hotels, restaurants, and marinas take advantage of the gorgeous views across the bay of downtown, Point Loma, and Coronado. Facing the island along the waterfront is Spanish Landing Park, which commemorates the 1769 meeting of the sea and land expeditions of Gaspar de Portolá and Junípero Serra (see p29) which permanently brought the Spanish to California. ⊗ Map B5

Marine Corps Recruit Depot

Listed on the National Register of Historic Places, the quaint Spanish-Colonial buildings were designed by Bertram Goodhue, architect of several buildings for the Panama-California Exposition in Balboa Park (see pp14–15). The Command Museum displays the history of the Marine Corps in Southern California and the wars in which they fought. Exhibits include photos, paintings, training films, weapons, and a World War II ambulance. ⊗ Map B4 • 1600 Henderson Ave • (619) 524-6719 • Open 8am–4pm Mon–Sat (photo ID for Depot; proof of insurance if driving)

Tent City

When John D. Spreckels acquired ownership of the Hotel del Coronado in 1890, he felt the beauty of the area should be available to everyone. He built "Tent City," a makeshift town that catered to the less-well-to-do. Arriving by rail and car, families paid $4.50 a week to live in tents equipped with beds, dressers, and flush toilets. Amenities included carnival booths, Japanese gardens, a library, and children's bull fights. At its peak, the town held 10,000 visitors. The tents came down by 1939, when they could no longer compete with the rising popularity of the roadside motel.

Sign up for DK's email newsletter on traveldk.com

Border Field State Park

As the endangered Western snowy plover seeks a place in which to lay her fragile eggs, the green-and-white vehicles of the US Border Patrol swoop down hillsides, lights blazing, in search of the illegal immigrant. An enormous, rusty, corrugated metal fence, which separates the US and Mexico, slices through the park before plunging into the sea. This southern part of the Tijuana River National Estuarine Research Reserve (see p47) attracts nature lovers who come to hike, ride horses, picnic on the beach, and birdwatch. On the Mexican side of the fence is a lively Mexican community and bullring (see p41).

Chula Vista Nature Center

The center is located in the Sweetwater Marsh National Wildlife Refuge, one of the few accessible salt marshes left on the Pacific Coast. Rent some binoculars and climb to an observation deck to see how many of the 200 bird species that inhabit the refuge you can spot. Or you can also take a self-guided tour along interpretative trails. Children will enjoy petting bat rays and leopard sharks. The parking lot is located near the Baysite/E Street Trolley Station; a free shuttle will take you to the center. ⊛ Map E3 • 1000 Gunpowder Point, Chula Vista • (619) 409-5900 • Open 9am–5pm daily • Adm

Border Field State Park

A Bike Ride Around Coronado

Morning

Begin at **Bikes & Beyond** (see p60) at the **Ferry Landing Market Place**. Walk to the sidewalk facing the harbor and enjoy the city view. Pedestrians and joggers also use this sidewalk, so proceed cautiously. Around the corner, you'll face the **Coronado Bridge** (see p24); the bougainvillea-covered walls on the right mark the **Marriott Resort** (see p114). Information boards on the way depict harbor wildlife and a map indicates the various navy yards. Under the bridge, the path turns away from the water. At the street, bear left and cross over. There is no protected bike path, but traffic is light on Glorietta Blvd.

At the marina, the road will fork; take the lower road to the left. Turn right at the stop-light and get off your bike; bike riding is forbidden on Orange Avenue. At 1025 Orange Avenue, **Moo Time Creamery** serves delicious homemade ice cream and smoothies. Walk your bike back to **Hotel del Coronado** (see p24) and check out the shops on its lower level (see p90). Leaving the hotel, bear left to Ocean Avenue; the Pacific Ocean is on the left and several mansions, built in the 1900s–1920s, are on the right. Turn right on Alameda and ride through a typical Coronado neighborhood with Spanish-style houses and bungalows. At 4th, cross the street and walk one block; the **Naval Air Station** will be on your left. Turn right on 1st. It's a straight stretch back to the Market Place.

Left **Shops at Ferry Landing Market Place** Right **Ocean Beach People's Organic Food Market**

Shops

Shops at the Hotel del Coronado

You'll find some of the best shopping in Coronado among these extensive shops in the hotel, including women's upscale casual wear, sunglasses, toys, jewelry, and the books of L. Frank Baum *(see p24)*.

Bay Books

This independent bookstore has helpful staff, an ample selection of books of local interest and international papers and magazines. ✆ *Map C6 • 1029 Orange Ave, Coronado • (619) 435-0070*

In Good Taste

A store that also operates a catering business, features select gourmet and entertainment items, as well as yummy chocolates. ✆ *Map C6 • 1146 Orange Ave, Coronado • (619) 425-8356*

Coronado Museum of History and Art Store

Head to this museum store for historic photos, posters, note cards, and books, as well as a fun selection of Wizard of Oz themed gifts *(see pp24–5)*.

Kippys

Specializing in "things that glitter," you'll find clothes with lots of sparkles for the rodeo, salsa dancing, or that upcoming pageant. For everyday wear, go for the embellished denim and leather. ✆ *Map C6 • 1114 Orange Ave, Coronado • (619) 435-6218*

Ferry Landing Market Place

Next to the Coronado Ferry dock *(see p25)*, this place offers an eclectic selection of souvenirs, clothing, and galleries. A great farmers' market sets up on Tuesday afternoons. ✆ *Map C6*

Newport Avenue

The main drag through Ocean Beach is chock full of antique shops. Some doorways front malls with dozens of shops inside. Finds range from 1950s retro to Victorian and Asian antiques. ✆ *Map B4 • Ocean Beach*

Ocean Beach People's Organic Food Market

This co-op market has been selling organic, minimally processed natural foods since 1971. For food to go, try the upstairs vegan deli. Non-members are welcome but will be charged a small percentage more. ✆ *Map B4 • 4765 Voltaire St • (619) 224-1387*

Orange Blossoms

Fun, color, and whimsy set the style here. Chic clothing and accessories for women, stylish fashions for girls, and beautiful baby clothes. ✆ *Map C6 • 952 Orange Ave, Coronado • (619) 437-8399*

The Shops at Las Americas

Within walking distance of the border with Mexico, you can stop by this immense outlet center before or after a trip to Tijuana. ✆ *Map E3 • San Ysidro*

Previous pages: **View of San Diego and the marina**

Price Categories

Price categories include	**$** under $20
a three-course meal for	**$$** $20–$40
one, half a bottle of wine,	**$$$** $40–$55
and all unavoidable extra	**$$$$** $55–$80
charges including tax.	**$$$$$** over $80

Hodad's

🔟 Places to Eat

1500 Ocean
The elegant atmosphere here is light and airy, as is the distinctive cuisine. There is also a good choice of wines from Southern California's finest vineyards. ✎ Map C6 • Hotel del Coronado, 1500 Orange Ave • (619) 435-6611 • $$$$$

Chez Loma
The luscious French cuisine will put you in heaven. Save with the early-bird special. ✎ Map C6 • 1132 Loma Ave, Coronado • (619) 435-0661 • Closed Mon • Limited dis. access • $$$$

Miguel's Cocina
Colorfully-dressed waitresses serve up enormous plates and lethal margaritas. The enchiladas, tacos, and burritos are hearty. ✎ Map C6 • 1351 Orange Ave, Coronado • (619) 437-4237 • $$

Primavera Ristorante
Legendary northern Italian cuisine is served here in an intimate setting. *Osso bucco* is the house specialty and the *tiramisu* is exceptional. ✎ Map C5 • 932 Orange Ave, Coronado • (619) 435-0454 • $$$$

Clayton's Coffee Shop
Old-fashioned, home-style cooking. A quarter buys three oldies at the jukebox. ✎ Map C6 • 979 Orange Ave • (619) 435-5425 • No dis. access • No credit cards • $

Hodad's
At a beach café devoted to burgers, brews, and surf, soak up the ambience self-described as junkyard Gothic. ✎ Map A4 • 5010 Newport Ave • (619) 224-4623 • $

Point Loma Seafoods
Order the freshest seafood in San Diego. Seafood salads and sushi are popular. ✎ Map B5 • 2805 Emerson St • (619) 223-1109 • $$

Café 1134
This café with a patio offers a selection of sandwiches, wraps, and panini. Breakfast is served all day. ✎ Map C6 • 1134 Orange Ave, Coronado • (619) 437-1134 • $

In-N-Out Burger
This fast food phenomenon relies only on burgers, fries, and drinks. Order "animal style," or "protein style" (a burger wrapped in lettuce). ✎ Map B4 • 3102 Sports Arena Blvd • (800) 786-1000 • $

Mistral
Enjoy memorable California-Mediterranean cuisine while looking out onto the bay. ✎ Map E2 • Loews Coronado Bay Resort, 4000 Coronado Bay Rd • (619) 424-4000 • $$$$

Unless otherwise stated, all restaurants are open daily, accept credit cards, serve vegetarian meals, and provide disabled access.

91

Left **Souvenirs at Avenida Revolución** Right **Mercado Hidalgo**

Shopping in Tijuana

Avenida Revolución
Keep a sense of humor, bargain hard, and remember: what you see is what you get. You may find some lovely folk art, a decent leather purse, and fine silver jewelry *(see p34)*.

Plaza Río Tijuana
Anchored by Dorian's department store, this large outdoor mall is the place for inexpensive clothes, shoes, and leather goods, and specialty and service shops. ◈ *Map E3 • Paseo de los Héroes*

Sanborn's
Tijuana's branch of the Mexico City department store and restaurant chain offers practical items for travelers, books, souvenirs, and folk art. The café is open for breakfast, lunch, and dinner. ◈ *Map E3 • Avenida Revolución, between calles 8 and 9*

Mercado Hidalgo
Strolling through Tijuana's open-air food market is an amazing education in exotic fruits, herbs, and chilies. Indoor shops sell housewares and the largest *piñata* collections ever seen. ◈ *Map E3 • Av Independencia at Blvd Sánchez Taboada*

Venus Fine Chocolates
This family-owned shop in front of the Caliente race track sells more than 20 flavors of delicious chocolate truffles with fillings such as caramel, nuts, and wine. ◈ *Map E3 • Av Tapachula*

Plaza Viva Tijuana
Within an easy walk from the American border, this large, modern mall offers restaurants, nightlife, and shops, but with fewer opportunities for bargaining than on Ave Revolución. ◈ *Map E3 • Paseo de los Héroes*

Pueblo Amigo Mall
A mix of clothing stores, bars, eateries, and a supermarket are combined at this Colonial-style outdoor mall located about 5 miles (8 km) from the border. ◈ *Map E3 • Vía Rápida Oriente 9211*

Plaza Agua Caliente
This upscale shopping mall offers several fine restaurants and many clothing and shoe stores. It is also a center for health and beauty, with day spas, gyms, and specialist treatments. ◈ *Map E3 • Blvd Agua Caliente 4558*

Silver
Genuine Mexican silverwork is lovely. By law, it must have four identifying marks: ".925," "Mexico," a tax identification number of the company, and the initials of the city of origin. Anything else is fake.

Farmacias
The hundreds of pharmacies in Tijuana cater mostly to Americans forced over the border by obscene US drug prices. You must have a prescription and can only bring back a reasonable personal amount.

Price Categories

Price categories include a three-course meal for one, half a bottle of wine, and all unavoidable extra charges including tax.

$	under $20
$$	$20–$40
$$$	$40–$55
$$$$	$55–$80
$$$$$	over $80

Café La Especial

🔟 Places to Eat in Tijuana

La Diferencia
A charming plant-filled and tiled hacienda offers gourmet choices such as shrimp *chile rellenos*, cactus salad, and seafood. ◈ *Map E3 • Blvd Sánchez Taboada 10521, Zona Río • (664) 634-3346 • $$*

Palmazul
Specializing in Baja California cuisine, Palmazul has a frequently changing selection of fresh seafood, poultry, and venison seasoned with the flavors of Baja. ◈ *Map E3 • Blvd Salinas 11154, Col Aviación • (664) 622-9773 • $$*

Café La Especial
Since 1952, patrons have eaten the *carne asada* – a thin filet of marinated grilled beef – savory tacos, and enchiladas with gusto. ◈ *Map E3 • Blvd Salinas 3600 • (664) 685-6654 • $*

Cien Años
The fine Mexican country dining here features traditional meat and seafood entrées, and exotic south-of-the-border dishes. More than 100 tequilas are on offer too. ◈ *Map E3 • Calle José María Velazco 2578 • (664) 634-3039 • $$$*

Chiki Jai
Spanish Jai Alai players from the Palacio Frontón (see p34) appreciated the Basque culinary specialties at this restaurant founded in 1947. Still Spanish-influenced, the food is delicious and well prepared. ◈ *Map E3 • Calle 7 • (664) 685-4955 • $$*

La Casa del Mole
The house specialty is *mole* sauce, which accompanies several meat dishes in this well-regarded restaurant. ◈ *Map E3 • Paseo de los Héroes 1051, Zona Río • (664) 634-6920 • No credit cards • $*

La Espadaña
The Spanish Mission-style dining room features mesquite-grilled meats, quail, and chicken filets. Breakfast here is one of the most popular in town. ◈ *Map E3 • Blvd Sánchez Taboada 10813, Zona Río • (664) 634-1488 • $*

La Fonda de Roberto
Traditional regional dishes from Mexico are served in this dining room with a courtyard. Entrées include meats with spicy *achiote* sauce, and *chile enogada*. ◈ *Map E3 • Blvd Cuauthémoc Sur Oriente 2800 • (664) 686-4687 • Closed Mon • $$*

La Escondida
A charming old hacienda and garden offers an excellent selection of international and Mexican cuisine, such as baby goat, roasted quail, and Châteaubriand. ◈ *Map E3 • Calle Santa Mónica 1, Las Palmas • (664) 681-4457 • $$*

La Cantina de los Remedios
Come here for traditional Mexican food accompanied by tequila or beer. This noisy restaurant has yellow walls, a ceiling mural, and bullfight posters. ◈ *Map E3 • Av Diego Rivera 2476 • (664) 634-3087 • $$*

Left **La Jolla's coastal view** Right **Feeding a giraffe at the Zoo Safari Park**

Northern San Diego

S AN DIEGO'S EXPLOSIVE GROWTH *has been concentrated in North County. With plenty of available land, prosperous hi-tech, biotech, commercial, and financial businesses have relocated here and now play a major role in the development of San Diego. Over one million people live in communities with distinct identities and attractions. Neighborhoods vary from the high-end rural estates of Rancho Santa Fe to the more modest housing of Marine Corps families in Oceanside. North County has wide-open spaces, rural charm, and geographical diversity to spare. From Camp Pendleton, travel past vast flower farms, avocado groves, and agricultural fields into mountain wilderness, and finish up in a spectacular desert.*

🔟 Sights

1. SeaWorld
2. La Jolla
3. San Diego Zoo Safari Park
4. Mission San Luis Rey de Francia
5. Temecula Wine Country
6. Julian
7. Anza-Borrego Desert State Park
8. Palomar Observatory
9. Pacific Beach
10. Mission Beach

Shipwreck rapids at SeaWorld

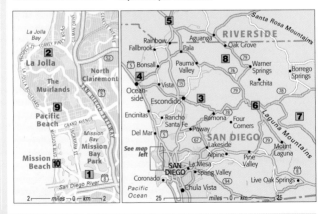

SeaWorld

Since 1964, SeaWorld has introduced over 100 million guests to marine life, with more than 35 attractions, exhibits, and shows. The park offers family-oriented thrill rides that compete with the numerous Southern California adventure parks. You can don a wetsuit and enter the dolphin pool in the Dolphin Interaction Program, or participate in Trainer For A Day, where you learn what it takes to be a killer whale and dolphin trainer. SeaWorld also hosts sleepovers, resident, and day camps (see pp30–31).

La Jolla

Spectacular and rich, with a gorgeous location and elegant restaurants and shops, this is an ideal destination. However, La Jollans do not sit around basking in their good fortune. Just north of the village along Torrey Pines Drive, some of the most prestigious research institutions in the world, many underwritten by La Jolla's residents, contribute to the good of humanity. Across the freeway, an area known as the Golden Triangle is a prosperous business and residential district with shops and restaurants (see pp32–3).

San Diego Zoo Safari Park

Many people prefer the Zoo Safari Park to its sister zoo in Balboa Park (see pp16–17). By monorail or a circuitous hiking trail, experience African and Asian animals roaming freely in enormous enclosures that replicate their natural environment. For the ultimate close-up encounter, reserve a spot on the photo caravan where an open-air

SeaWorld Adventure Camp complex

truck takes you into the animal habitats. A successful breeding program has brought 125 cheetahs, 142 rhinos, and nearly extinct California condors and Arabian oryxes into the world. ◈ Map E2 • 15500 San Pasqual Valley Rd, Escondido • (760) 747-8702 • Open Jan–mid-Jun & mid-Sep–mid-Dec: 9am–4pm daily; mid-Jun–mid-Sep & mid-Dec–Dec 31: 9am–8pm daily • Adm

Mission San Luis Rey de Francia

Named after canonized French king Louis IX, this mission was the last to be established in Southern California. Franciscan padres oversaw enormous tracts of land devoted to cattle, sheep, and horses, and a Native American population of 2,800. Relations between the missionaries and the indigenous population were so successful that when Father Peyri was ordered by the Mexican government to return to Spain in 1832, the Native Americans followed him to San Diego Harbor. Today's restored mission offers displays on life and artifacts of the mission era. Still administered by Franciscan friars, the mission offers popular retreats. ◈ Map D1 • 4050 Mission Ave, Oceanside • (760) 757-3651 (ext. 117) • Open 9am–5pm Mon–Fri, 10am–5pm Sat & Sun • Adm • www.sanluisrey.org

Statue at Mission San Luis Rey de Francia

5 Temecula Wine Country

During the mission days, Franciscan friars recognized that San Diego's soil and climate were ideal for planting grape vines. However, it wasn't until the 1960s that wine was first produced commercially. Now over two dozen wineries stretch across rolling hills studded with oak trees, most of them along Rancho California Road. Wineries offer tastings for a small fee, and many of them operate restaurants and delis. Two of the most popular wineries in the area are Thornton Winery and Callaway Vineyard & Winery.

Map E1 • Thornton Winery: 32575 Rancho California Rd • (951) 699-0099 • Callaway Vineyard & Winery: 32720 Rancho California Rd • (951) 676-4001

6 Julian

When Fred Coleman discovered gold here in 1869, scores of prospectors poured into the region. The boom was over in less than five years, but some stayed on in this charming little community surrounded by oak and pine forests high in the Cuyamaca Mountains. Now this designated Historical District is filled with B&Bs, and it is a popular weekend getaway. Julian is also well known for its apple orchards (see p41).

7 Anza-Borrego Desert State Park

Fantastic geological formations, archeological sites, and sweeping desert vistas are only a backdrop for the wildlife found in the largest state park in California. Golden eagles soar above, road-runners dart across the paths, and bighorn sheep dot the mountainsides.

Palomar Observatory at sunset

In springtime, a dazzling array of wildflowers create a magic show of colors across the desert. Stop by the visitor center to pick up a map that marks hiking trails, sites of Native American pictographs, and the park's best viewpoints. Map F2

THORNTON WINERY

Thornton Winery logo

8 Palomar Observatory

High atop one of North County's highest mountains, the dome of the observatory has an otherworldly look. Part of the California Institute of Technology, Palomar is home to the 200-in (508-cm) Hale Telescope, the largest optical instrument of its kind when installed in 1947. Its moving parts weigh 530 tons, the mirror 14.5 tons. Thanks to computer technology, no one

---

Brain Power

Beneath San Diego's image of "fun in the sun" is one of the country's most highly educated populations. San Diego has one of the highest PhDs per capita in the nation, 30 percent hold college degrees, and 20 percent of the county's adults are involved in higher education. La Jolla boasts some of the most prestigious research facilities: the Salk Institute, Scripps Research Institute, Scripps Institution of Oceanography, and UCSD.

"looks" through the telescope anymore. Self-guided tours offer a look at the telescope itself; on some Saturdays and Sundays, there are also docent-led tours for a fee. ◎ *Map E1 • 35899 Canfield Road, Palomar Mountain • (760) 742-2119 • Open 9am–3pm daily (until 4pm Apr–Oct) • Free*

Pacific Beach
Residents here enjoy an endless summer climate and an easy-going lifestyle. Life revolves around Garnet Avenue, lined with nightclubs, cafés, late-night restaurants, and shops. The street ends at the 1927 Crystal Pier, a great location to watch surfers, catch a fish, or spend the night in a tiny cottage. Come early to claim a fire ring on the beach and cook up some marshmallows, or bicycle along the boardwalk to Mission Beach *(see p65)*.

Mission Beach
The California beach scene struts in full glory along a narrow strip of land filled with vacation rentals and beachwear shops. Skaters, cyclists, and joggers whiz along the Strand, while surfers, volleyball devotees, and sun worshippers pack the sand. Sometimes the streets become so crowded on the Fourth of July weekend that the police have to shut the area down. A block away, Belmont Park *(see p52)* is an old-fashioned fun zone with a vintage roller coaster *(see p64)*.

Mission Beach

A Walk in La Jolla

Morning

🕐 Begin by looking out the front door of the landmark **Hotel La Valencia** *(see p115)*. Turn left onto Prospect Street and walk past restaurants and art galleries. Before you reach Coast Boulevard, a stairway to the left leads to the **Sunny Jim Cave**. Steps lead through a tunnel into a fascinating, ocean-carved cave, named by L. Frank Baum *(see p39)*. To the left of the entrance a platform overlooks the caves. Continue along Coast Boulevard, admiring views of **Torrey Pines** and **Scripps Pier**. Pass through **Ellen Browning Scripps Park** *(see p46)*. Beyond the end of the park is **Children's Pool** *(see p53)*. Check out the seals and sea lions. Turn left on Cuvier Street and left onto Prospect Street. You'll now be at the **Museum of Contemporary Art** *(see p32)*. Check out the exhibits or have a snack in the café. Louis Gill designed the original museum and the older architecture in this area. Walk back toward the village and peek inside **780 Prospect St**; the cottage dates back to 1904. Cross Prospect at Fay but keep on Prospect. Pass through the Arcade Building to Girard Avenue. Turn right and window-shop along La Jolla's main street. Of note is **Warwick's** at 7812, a stationer and bookstore, and **R. B. Stevenson Gallery** *(see p99)*. Go north on Girard for a block and a half. Time to enjoy the freshly baked delights at locals' favorite, **Girard Gourmet** *(see p101)*.

Left **Solana Beach** Right **Miniature urban scene at Legoland**

TOP 10 North County Highway 101

Del Mar
The wealthiest community among North County's beach towns, Del Mar is filled with sidewalk cafés, restaurants, and boutiques. ✎ Map D2

Solana Beach
At one of North County's most popular beach towns, Fletcher Cove Beach Park is perfect for swimming and walking. ✎ Map D2

Cardiff-by-the-Sea
Surfers enjoy the reef break at Cardiff, while RV campers kick back at a beachside campground. The San Elijo Lagoon offers hiking trails through an ecological reserve. ✎ Map D2

Encinitas
Voted one of the "Top 10 Surf Towns in the US" by *Surfer* magazine, local highlights include the Self-Realization Fellowship Retreat and Hermitage and the San Diego Botanic Garden. ✎ Map D2 • Self-Realization Fellowship Retreat and Hermitage: 215 W K St • San Diego Botanic Garden: 230 Quail Gardens Dr • Adm

Leucadia
The 21st century hasn't yet hit this sleepy little town with a small beach and a few shops, restaurants, and galleries. ✎ Map D2

The Flower Fields
In spring, the hillsides explode with brilliant-colored blossoms of the giant tecolote ranunculus. The Carlsbad Ranch harvests 6–8 million bulbs for export. ✎ Map D1 • 5704 Paseo del Norte, Carlsbad • Adm

Legoland
This theme park and aquarium is devoted to the plastic brick. Kids enjoy the hands-on activities, rides, and models *(see p52)*.

Carlsbad
In the 1880s, Captain John Frazier discovered that the water here had the same mineral content as a spa in Karlsbad, Bohemia. Today, this pretty village still draws visitors with its beaches, resorts, and shops. ✎ Map D1

Oceanside
Town fortunes are tied inevitably with adjoining Camp Pendleton. The California Surf Museum presents a history of the sport. ✎ Map D1 • California Surf Museum: 312 Pier View Way • (760) 721-6876 • Open 10am–4pm daily

Camp Pendleton
Several endangered species and abundant wildlife thrive at the largest US Marine Corps base and amphibious training facility in the country. ✎ Map D1

Left **Lucy** Right **Sign for Cedros Design District**

🔟 Shopping

1 Lucy
This women's clothing store sells a large selection of good-quality active wear for yoga, running, and the gym, as well as casual clothing for outdoor pursuits and traveling. ✆ *Map N3 • 7868 Girard Ave, La Jolla • (858) 729-1897*

2 R. B. Stevenson Gallery
Local, Californian, national, and international artists all feature in the changing exhibitions at this light, spacious gallery of contemporary abstract art and sculpture. ✆ *Map N3 • 7661 Girard Ave, La Jolla • (858) 459-3917*

3 Ascot Shop
Men who are looking for a quality tailored jacket and conservative casual wear will find a wide selection at this upscale store. ✆ *Map N3 • 7750 Girard Ave, La Jolla • (858) 454-4222*

4 My Own Space
Dedicated to personal style, this fun shop offers a variety of modern classics and original furnishings, as well as accessories for the home. ✆ *Map N3 • 7840 Girard Ave, La Jolla • (858) 459-0099*

5 Pilar's Beachwear
There's no excuse to be without a swimsuit. Pilar's large selection of domestic and imported bikinis, one-pieces, and cover-ups, suitable for every age and body type, are in stock. ✆ *Map A3 • 3790 Mission Blvd, Mission Beach (858) 488-3056*

6 Trader Joe's
This market sells imaginative salads, a wide variety of cheeses, wine, and fun ethnic food that you won't find in a regular supermarket. ✆ *Map A3 • 1211 Garnet Ave, Pacific Beach • (858) 272-7235*

7 Carlsbad Premium Outlets
Shop for bargains in one of the most pleasant outlet centers around. The Gap, Bass, Salvatore Ferragamo, and Jones New York are all here. ✆ *Map D1 • 5620 Paseo del Norte, Carlsbad*

8 Cedros Design District
This former warehouse district has transformed into a shopping street full of design stores, furnishings, and boutiques. The 100 shops at the Leaping Lotus offer ethnic goods, clothing, and furniture. ✆ *Map D2 • Cedros Ave, Solana Beach*

9 Del Mar Plaza
Italian home accessories, estate art, and well-known chains such as Banana Republic and White House/Black Market cater to the discriminating. ✆ *Map D2 • 1555 Camino Del Mar, Del Mar*

10 Winery Gift Shops
Most wineries in Temecula operate gift shops that stock unusual cookbooks, entertaining supplies, and home decor items. Additionally, many have delis where you can find picnic food to accompany that bottle of wine you just bought. ✆ *Map E1*

Left **Wild Note Café** Right **Brockton Villa**

🔟 Cafés & Bars

Coyote Bar & Grill
Southwestern and Mexican-style appetizers and an extensive tequila menu keep this singles' hunting ground jumping. 🗺 Map D1 • 300 Carlsbad Village Dr, Carlsbad • (760) 729-4695 • $$

Belly Up Tavern
Considered one of the best live music venues in the county, old Quonset huts have been acoustically altered to showcase almost famous and famous bands. 🗺 Map D2 • 143 S. Cedros Ave, Solana Beach • (858) 481-9022 • Adm

Wild Note Café
Come here for lunch: salads and sandwiches are served outside or under ornamented and painted structural beams. Concert-goers from the Belly Up Tavern make dinners hectic. 🗺 Map D2 • 143 S. Cedros Ave, Solana Beach • (858) 720-9000 • $$

Brockton Villa
This historic place offers breakfast, lunch, or dinner, and fabulous views. Choices include crab salad, seafood, and steak. 🗺 Map N2 • 1235 Coast Blvd, La Jolla • (858) 454-7393 • No dis. access • $$$

Pannikin
You can't miss this coffee-house located inside a historic Santa Fe Railroad Depot. Grab a beverage and sit upstairs or outside on a shady deck. 🗺 Map D2 • 510 N. Coast Hwy 101, Leucadia • (760) 436-5824 • $

Living Room Coffeehouse
If you're looking for a place to use your laptop, try this hip coffeehouse in upscale La Jolla. Grab a back table to enjoy that million-dollar view. 🗺 Map N2 • 1010 Prospect St • (858) 459-1187 • $

Ruby's Diner
Walk 1,942 ft (591 m) out to the pier's end and reward yourself with a salad, Santa Fe or traditional burger, and a malt at this 1940s-style diner. 🗺 Map D1 • 1 Oceanside Pier, Oceanside • (760) 433-7829 • $

Zinc Café
Great coffee, pastries, and a wide selection of vegetarian dishes make this cozy café a good choice for a shopping break at the Cedros Design Center. 🗺 Map D2 • 132 S. Cedros Ave, Solana Beach • (858) 793-5436 • $

Dudley's Bakery
Boasting an almost cult-like popularity, everyone stops in this bakery and snack shop near Julian. Lines are long to buy loaves of 18 varieties of bread. 🗺 Map E2 • 30218 Hwy 78 & 79, Santa Ysabel • (760) 765-0488 • $

Lean and Green Café
Enjoy a wide spread of fresh, organic food and drinks, which includes wraps, salads, sandwiches, and smoothies. Many vegan and gluten-free items are also available. 🗺 Map N3 • 7825 Fay Ave, 180 La Jolla • (858) 459-5326 • $

Unless otherwise stated, all restaurants are open daily, accept credit cards, serve vegetarian meals, and provide disabled access.

Roppongi

Price Categories

Price categories include a three-course meal for one, half a bottle of wine, and all unavoidable extra charges including tax.

$	under $20
$$	$20–$40
$$$	$40–$55
$$$$	$55–$80
$$$$$	over $80

🔟 Places to Eat

George's at the Cove
Whether you dine on the terrace or in the dining room, the service, food, and ocean views are always superb. ◈ *Map P2 • 1250 Prospect St • (858) 454-4244 • $$$ (terrace) • $$$$$ (dining room)*

Osteria Romantica
Authentic Italian cuisine in a cheerful restaurant. Checkered tablecloths, painted chairs, and tile floors create a welcoming atmosphere. ◈ *Map Q2 • 2151 Avenida de la Playa • (858) 551-1221 • $$$*

Roppongi
Pacific Rim tapas, such as Mongolian shredded duck quesadillas, make this place special. ◈ *Map N3 • 875 Prospect St • (858) 551-5252 • $$$$*

101 Café
Since its 1928 beginnings as a roadside diner, celebrities and folks just passing through have enjoyed the home-style comfort food. ◈ *Map D1 • 631 S. Coast Hwy, Oceanside • (760) 722-5220 • $*

The Cottage
At this lovely, quiet 1900s bungalow, the patio is the perfect place to enjoy a light breakfast or lunch. ◈ *Map N3 • 7702 Fay Ave • (858) 454-8409 • $$*

Girard Gourmet
Select from salads, entrées, and sandwiches. Designer cookies are a specialty. ◈ *Map N2 • 7837 Girard Ave • (858) 454-3321 • $*

Sushi Ota
Considered the best sushi in town, connoisseurs come for the day's freshest fish transformed into tasty works of art. ◈ *Map B3 • 4529 Mission Bay Dr • (858) 270-5670 • $$$$*

Rubio's
As the first of a hugely successful Mexican fast-food chain, enjoy the best fish tacos this side of Baja. ◈ *Map B3 • 4504 E. Mission Bay Dr • (858) 272-2801 • $*

Mille Fleurs
The most acclaimed restaurant in San Diego County is a culinary feast. Fireplaces, fresh flowers, and tapestries complement the exquisite and beautifully presented food. ◈ *Map E2 • 6009 Paseo Delicias, Rancho Santa Fe • (858) 756-3085 • $$$$$*

Julian Café & Bakery
Home-style cooking in a Western atmosphere attracts locals and weekenders. The food isn't really memorable, but you won't forget the cowboy memorabilia. ◈ *Map F2 • 2112 Main St • (760) 765-2712 • No dis. access • $*

Following pages: **Horton Plaza in downtown San Diego**

STREETSMART

SAN DIEGO'S TOP 10

Left **Tourist Office** Right **Gay and lesbian newspaper stands**

Planning Your Trip

Tourist Offices
Multilingual staff at the International Visitors Information Center can answers queries on activities and accommodation, and also sell tickets to attractions. Ask for a copy of the *San Diego Visitors Planning Guide*. The Mission Bay Visitor Information Center is handy if you're driving on the I-5 and need help with accommodation. The Coronado Visitors Center can give you a map of Coronado and suggest activities in the area.

Media
The *San Diego Reader* is the best source of the latest happenings in town. You'll find restaurant reviews, movies and theater timings, and music events. Free copies can be found throughout the city.

Internet
Websites offer useful information about package vacations, current events, new attractions, city services, transportation, sports, parks, and restaurants in San Diego.

Maps
Maps from the tourist information offices are good for basic sightseeing. To explore San Diego further, Auto Club maps give a good overview, or buy comprehensive street maps of the county published by Thomas Bros.

Visas
International travelers should check with their US embassy for visa information as this is subject to change. Travelers visiting under the Visa Waiver Program must register at https://esta.cbp.dhs.gov before departure. There is an administration fee. US and Canadian citizens, as well as other travelers visiting Tijuana for the day, need a passport.

Insurance
Be sure to get comprehensive travel insurance before arriving in the US, or expect large bills even if you aren't denied medical care. If renting a car, establish what your auto insurer and credit card company covers in case of accident or theft. An auto insurance policy is not valid in Mexico; buy Mexican insurance at the border.

When to Go
San Diego enjoys the most temperate climate in the nation. The rainy season usually begins in December, with a few large storms rolling in by spring. Winter days can be warm and sunny, but ocean temperatures are cold. Summer showers are mild, and evenings are pleasant.

What to Take
Casual dress is the rule. Evenings can be cool, so tuck in a sweater or lightweight jacket.

How Long to Stay
Depending on your stamina, San Diego's sights can be covered in a week or less. SeaWorld and the Zoo tend to be exhausting all-day affairs, so plan a light day after your visits. Allow a few days to travel up the coast or around the backcountry.

Traveling with Children
San Diego is a nonstop kids' playground. Hotels welcome families, although some B&Bs are not set up for children. Many of the larger resorts feature kids programs and can supply names of licensed babysitters.

Directory

Tourist Offices
• *International Visitors Information Center: (619) 236-1212*
• *Mission Bay Visitor Information Center: (619) 276-8200*
• *Coronado Visitors Center: (619) 437-8788*

San Diego Reader
• *www.sandiegoreader. com*

San Diego Websites
• *www.sandiego.org*
• *www.sandiego.gov*
• *www.signonsan diego.com*

Auto Club Maps
• *AAA office: 2440 Hotel Cir N, Mission Valley*

Department of State
• *http://travel.state.gov*

Left **San Diego International Airport, Lindbergh Field** Right **Greyhound Bus**

🔟 Getting to San Diego

San Diego International Airport – Lindbergh Field

Most flights land at Terminals 1 and 2, with Southwest Airlines located in Terminal 1. Short flights within Southern California operate from the Commuter Terminal. The only non-stop international flights fly to and from Mexico and Canada.

Getting into Town

Exiting Terminals 1 and 2, the skybridge links to the Transportation Plaza. Flyer Route 992 is a public bus that departs every 10 minutes from 5am to 12:50am and connects with the trolley and Amtrak before continuing up Broadway. Many hotels are only 10 minutes away.

Private Shuttles, Taxis, & Limo Services

Door-to-door shuttles are available at the airport's Transportation Plaza. Fares are based on distance and per person. Limo services can meet you in baggage claim. Call ahead to book a pickup to the airport.

Aeropuerto Internacional General Abelardo L. Rodríguez – Tijuana

Located 5 miles (8 km) east of downtown, frequent flights link Tijuana to the rest of Mexico. Domestic flights within Mexico are often cheaper than flying internationally from California.

Customs

Each person above 21 is allowed one liter of liquor and 200 cigarettes duty free. Citizens may bring in $400 worth of gifts, non-citizens $100. Cash exceeding $10,000 must be declared. Fresh produce, meats, and plants are prohibited.

Cruise Ships

All cruise ships moor at B Street Terminal along the Embarcadero on N. Harbor Drive. Ships sail to the Mexican Riviera or do mini-cruises to Ensenada and Catalina.

Amtrak Trains

Amtrak's Pacific Surf-liners arrive at the historic Santa Fe Depot. About eleven trains travel daily to and from Orange County and Los Angeles, and several continue on to Santa Barbara.

Greyhound Buses

Greyhound buses operate 24 hours, are air conditioned, cheap, and cover the entire US and most of Canada. There are direct connections to LA, Las Vegas, and Phoenix, and buses from downtown to Tijuana's central bus terminal.

Car

From Los Angeles, I-5 passes along coastal towns, heads into downtown, and continues to the international border. Shortly before La Jolla, I-5 splits with I-805, re-connecting at the border. If coming from the east, I-8 passes through Mission Valley and ends just past SeaWorld. I-15 from Las Vegas serves inland San Diego County.

McClellan-Palomar Airport

This airport is useful if visiting North County. Some 30-miles (48-km) north of downtown, United Express flies shuttles to and from Los Angeles. Parking costs $3 per day and is limited to 30 days.

Directory

Airports
• *San Diego International Airport: (619) 400-2900*
• *Tijuana International Airport: (664) 607-8200*
• *McClellan-Palomar Airport: (760) 431-4646*

Shuttles, Taxis, & Limo Services
• *Cloud 9 Shuttle: (800) 974-8885 toll free*
• *Yellow Cab of San Diego: (858) 444-4444*
• *La Costa Limousines: (888) 299-5466 toll free*

Amtrak Buses
• *Santa Fe Depot: 1050 Kettner Blvd; (800) 872-7245*

Greyhound Buses
• *120 W. Broadway; (619) 239-3266*

Taxis charge by the car, so for three or four people a taxi may be cheaper than the airport shuttle.

Left **Detail of trolley sign** Center **Taxi** Right **Cyclists on Embarcadero**

TOP 10 Getting Around San Diego

Trolley
Inexpensive and fun, this light-rail system has three lines. The Blue line travels between Old Town, downtown, and San Ysidro. The Orange line is handy for the Gaslamp Quarter, the Convention Center, and Seaport Village. The Green line travels between Old Town and Santee. Tickets are available at station vending machines, and are good for buses too.

Buses
Buses connect with the North County Transit District, which serves coastal and inland San Diego County. Fares are payable in exact change as you board. The Transit Store offers maps and the *Fun Places to Go!* brochure, which details how to reach sights by bus.

The Coaster
A regional rail service runs between downtown and Oceanside, stopping in Old Town, Sorrento Valley, Solana Beach, Encinitas, Carlsbad, and Oceanside. Trains run Monday to Saturday. Buy tickets at a vending machine and validate them before boarding.

Ferry
A fun way to travel to Coronado is on the San Diego–Coronado Ferry. It takes passengers and bicycles only. Buy your ticket at the San Diego Harbor Excursion Dock or the Ferry Landing Market Place in Coronado. Ferries leave San Diego at 9am and run hourly until 9pm, Sun–Thu, and an hour later Fri–Sat.

Cars
You won't need a car if you're only visiting downtown, but it's essential to get quickly around the rest of the city. A few car rental agencies have cars you can drive into Mexico. Don't forget to buy additional insurance at the border.

Taxis
Taxis don't cruise for fares. You can usually find one in front of large hotels, the airport, or some shopping centers. Rates are clearly posted on the taxi door; distances in San Diego can make some trips an expensive proposition.

Harbor Cruises
San Diego Harbor Excursion offers several ways to tour the harbor. One- and two-hour narrated trips cover the harbor, Shelter Island, Point Loma, Coronado Bridge, and more. Sunday brunch, dinner, nature and whale-watching cruises are also available.

Limousines
For a touch of luxury, limousines can be hired for one-way and round-trip transfers, or for the day. Drivers can provide good insider information.

Excursions
Old Town Trolley Tours circle Old Town, Seaport Village, Horton Plaza, Balboa Park, the Zoo, and Coronado. You can get on or off all day; the full circuit takes two hours. Gray Line San Diego offers narrated tours of the city, as well as day trips to Southern California theme parks and Mexico.

San Diego Water Taxi
On-call water taxis will transport you to locations around the harbor. They run from 9am to 9pm Sunday to Thursday, and 9am to 11pm on Friday and Saturday.

Directory

MTS Trolley & Buses
• (619) 231-1466;
www.transit.511sd.com

Taxis, Limousines & Water Taxis
• San Diego Cab: (619) 226-8294 • Yellow Cab: (858) 444-4444 • Coronado Cab: (619) 435-6211 • La Costa Limousine: (760) 438-4455 • San Diego Water Taxi: (619) 235-8294

Harbor Cruises
• San Diego Harbor Excursion: 1050 N. Harbor Dr; (619) 234-4111

Excursions
• Old Town Trolley Tours: (619) 298-8687
• Gray Line San Diego: (800) 331-5077

Left **Cars queue up at the Mexico-Tijuana border** Right **Lifeguard vehicles**

TOP 10 Things to Avoid

1 Driving Frustrations

Morning and afternoon rush hour on Interstates is an appalling exercise in futility. A 30-minute drive on the I-5 can take hours. Ask someone at your hotel how to time things, and know your directions well. Parking in Mission Beach or La Jolla can be next to impossible in the summer.

2 Car Theft

San Diego's proximity to the Mexican border makes car theft a concern. Even if your car is found across the border, the paperwork to bring it back is a nightmare. Neighborhoods prone to theft include Pacific Beach, San Ysidro, and Mission Valley.

3 Driving Without Insurance in Mexico

If your car is stolen while over the border, your US car insurance won't cover it. If you are in any way associated with an accident, your vehicle will be impounded and you will be arrested until liability is sorted out. Protect yourself by buying a policy before driving over the border.

4 Narcotraficantes

Narcotraficantes, or drug smugglers, thrive along the border with the local drug cartel. In 2008, a clamp-down in Tijuana resulted in open conflict between drug dealers and law enforcement, which still continues today. Visit the US State Department website (http://tijuana.usconsulate.gov) for current travel conditions. Visitors to Mexico should use common sense and limit explorations to popular tourist areas when travel advisories are in place.

5 Sun

Slather on the sunscreen during the day and be sure to take a hat whenever you're outdoors, especially at SeaWorld and the Zoo. California has one of the country's highest incidences of skin cancer; no surprise since people pursue outdoor activities year round.

6 High Surf

Dangerous riptides can occur along the coastal beaches; ask the lifeguards about swimming conditions at an unfamiliar beach. Posted green flags indicate safe swimming, yellow mean caution, and red flags denote hazardous surf. If you are caught in a riptide, let the current carry you down the coast until it dies out, and then swim in to the shore.

7 Water Contamination

Ocean waters are generally clean, except after a heavy storm. Accumulated and untreated runoff from miles away washes down storm drains and empties into the ocean, and sewer leaks are common. Especially hard-hit beaches are Imperial Beach and Border Field State Park. There are signs indicating safety levels of the water.

8 Smoking

Smoking is forbidden inside any public enclosed area, including restaurants and bars, although a few establishments have designated smoking patios. The city of San Diego has banned smoking on beaches, in parks, and in open spaces; some communities are trying to forbid smoking on streets. It's possible to spend your entire vacation in San Diego without smelling a single cigarette.

9 Panhandlers

Like any major city, San Diego has its share of panhandlers, most of whom are not aggressive. Downtown has the largest concentration, followed by the beach towns, including La Jolla.

10 Crime

San Diego is a safe city; most petty crime is limited to theft and car break-ins. Common sense prevails: don't walk around late at night; don't leave valuables inside your car; and don't give an angry salute to a driver who's cutting you off.

Left **San Diego Museum of Art, Balboa Park** Right **Rose Garden at Balboa Park**

🔟 Budget Tips

1 Airline Deals
When flying into Southern California, consider an open-jaw ticket, with which you can fly into Los Angeles and depart from San Diego. Two good budget airlines are Southwest Airlines and JetBlue.

2 Hotel Discounts
Discounts are offered to Auto Club members, military personnel, corporate employees, and retirees. The best online prices and rooms are usually on the hotel's own website. Contacting the hotel directly might find you a lower rate.

3 Free Museum Days
Every museum in Balboa Park offers free entry on one Tuesday each month to their permanent exhibits; special traveling exhibits or programs still charge admission. The Museum of Contemporary Art in La Jolla and in downtown San Diego is free 5–7pm every third Thursday every month.

4 Coupons
Stop by the tourist brochure racks at hotels, restaurants, and visitor centers to pick up discount coupons for museums, SeaWorld, the Zoo, car rentals, hotels, and restaurants. Promotional coupons can often be found in Sunday papers and the *San Diego Reader* (see p104).

5 Entertainment & Attractions For Free
Unwind in Balboa Park, daydream in the lobby of Hotel del Coronado, or hang out on the Mission Beach boardwalk. Hear a free Sunday concert at the Spreckels Organ Pavilion. Check out the local talent in cafés and bars. Walkabout International organizes free daily walking tours.

6 Parking
Many hotels operate shuttles to SeaWorld and other attractions. Parking at the Zoo, Balboa Park, and Old Town is free, as well as at many trolley stops. At Westfield Horton Plaza, buy anything and receive a few hours of validated parking. At the Tijuana border, park for free on the street in front of the outlet center.

7 Gasoline
San Diego has some of the highest gas prices in the US. If you fill up in La Jolla or along the freeways, you'll be broke. Look for stations away from the coast and tourist attractions; Arco stations tend to be the lowest priced.

8 Multiple Theme Park Passes
The "Passport to Balboa Park Combo" includes the Zoo and park museums for a set number of days. Other packages include variations of the Zoo, Zoo Safari Park, and SeaWorld. The "Go San Diego Card" includes the Zoo, Zoo Safari Park, Legoland, and many other attractions.

9 Arts Tix
Tickets for music, dance, and theater performances throughout the San Diego area are available for half price at a kiosk in front of Westfield Horton Plaza. A small service fee is charged.

10 Transportation Passes
Stop by the Transit Store to pick up a transit pass good for buses of the Metropolitan Transit System, the North County Transit District, and the San Diego Trolley. Passes are available for 14 and 30 days, and there are premium monthly passes too.

Directory

Airlines
• Southwest Airlines: (800) 435-9792
• JetBlue: (800) 538-2583

Walkabout International
• (619) 231-7463

Arts Tix
• (858) 381-5595

Transportation Passes
• Transit Store: www.sdcommute.com

Left **Disabled sign at hotel entrance** Right **Disabled-friendly trolley**

🔟 Special Needs Tips

Disabled Parking
Reserved parking spaces are marked by a blue curb, a blue-and-white wheelchair logo on the pavement, and by a posted sign. You may also park with no charge at any regular parking metered area. A special disabled permit must be displayed at all times. The process for obtaining a permit takes at least a month.

Hotels & Restaurants
Hotels with over five rooms must provide accessible accommodation to disabled guests. Always call in advance to reserve one of these rooms, and specify if you need a roll-in shower. When making restaurant reservations, do clarify that you require access.

Transportation
All buses, the San Diego Trolley, and the Coaster are equipped with lifts. Amtrak trains have limited accessible spaces and recommend advance reservations. Greyhound provides a lift-equipped bus with advance notice. The Cloud 9 super shuttle provides transportation from the airport, also with advance notice.

Accessible San Diego
The excellent booklet *Access In San Diego* gives specific access information on many hotels, restaurants, and shopping centers. Also included are tour bus companies, public and private transportation firms equipped with lifts, and car rental agencies that offer hand-controlled vehicles. You'll also find a directory of medical equipment suppliers and disability organizations.

Power Beach Chairs
Imperial Beach, Mission Beach, Coronado, Oceanside, and Silver Strands have power and manual beach chairs, while Ocean Beach and La Jolla offer manual chairs. Advance reservations and ID are required. You must be able to get into and out of the chair.

Ramped Curbs
Every intersection and sidewalk in San Diego has ramped curbs or at least a ramped driveway. Ramped access is standard in government buildings, universities, concert halls, museums, some theaters, and large hotels and restaurants.

Accessible Toilets
The universal wheelchair symbol indicates restrooms that are private unisex or single occupancy with locking doors.

San Diego Zoo
The park map indicates walkways where you may need extra assistance if your mobility is limited or you're in a wheelchair.
Have an employee call for shuttle assistance if you need it. Regular and motorized wheelchairs are available for rent near the zoo entrance.

Balboa Park
Older buildings are now in compliance for disabled access. Free park trams have been equipped with wheelchair lifts, and most restrooms are wheelchair accessible. For those with special needs and with advanced arrangement, the education office of most museums can supply a staff member to escort and narrate tours.

Tijuana
No federal law in Mexico requires businesses to provide disabled access. Many curbs in Tijuana are ramped, but the drawback is the poor condition of the sidewalks. Yet, many mobility-impaired people do successfully navigate the streets.

Directory

Cloud 9 super shuttle
• *(800) 974-8885*

Accessible San Diego
• *(619) 325-7550; www.asd.travel*

Disabled Parking Permits
• *http://dmv.ca.gov/ pubs/brochures/fast_ facts/ffvr07.htm*

Beach Wheelchairs
• *Imperial (619) 685-7972; www.coastal. ca.gov.access/beaches*

Left **Fire Engine** Center **Pharmacy sign** Right **Women's restroom sign**

TOP 10 Security & Health

1 Consulates
Some European consuls only deal with trade issues; they do not issue passports or visas. In an emergency, contact your embassy in Washington, DC or LA. Dial 411 for assistance.

2 If You Lose Everything
Before leaving home, it is advisable to photocopy all important papers. If you lose your wallet, make a police report, notify your credit card companies, and notify the credit-reporting companies to prevent identity theft. You can have money wired through Western Union.

3 911
During an emergency, dial this number free from any telephone. Be prepared to specify if medical and/or police assistance is needed and your location. Call the police department for all other matters.

4 Hospitals
San Diego has some of the country's best hospitals. If your situation is not life threatening, urgent care clinics are less expensive. Call your insurance company for a referral to a local doctor or clinic.

5 Pharmacies
CVS and Rite-Aid have 24-hour pharmacies.

6 Helplines
If you don't have health insurance, head to a community clinic. Expect to pay on the spot for services rendered. Look in the Yellow Pages under "clinics" to find a walk-in clinic.

7 If You're in a Car Accident
Call 911 if anyone is injured. Call the police if property damage appears to be over $500 and/or you need a police report. Drivers must exchange driver's license information and all vehicle insurance details. If you're in a rental car, report any accidents or vehicle damage to the agency immediately.

8 Seatbelts
It is California law for all passengers in the car to wear seatbelts. If not, you can be pulled over by the police and ticketed. Children under six and who weigh less than 60 lbs (27 kg) must be secured in a car safety seat. If renting a car, make a request to the agency for a child seat in advance.

9 Public Restrooms
All major attractions have restrooms, as do gas stations and restaurants. Shopping centers, public buildings, libraries, and large hotels are other places to try. Beach restrooms are an option if you can't find a better alternative.

10 Food & Water Safety
All restaurants must post a letter grade, indicating the sanitation level. An "A" means the restaurant has passed inspection; a "B" is passing, but sanitation issues exist; with a "C," a restaurant has 30 days to improve or risk closure. Water from the faucet is safe to drink but may not taste great.

Directory

Consulates
• *Consulate General of Mexico: (619) 231-8414*
• *British Consulate, La Jolla: (858) 459-8231*
• *US Consulate, Tijuana: (664) 622-7400*
• *For other foreign consulates in San Diego: www.embassy. goabroad.com*

Emergency Numbers
• *Medical or police assistance: 911*
• *San Diego Police Department (non-emergency): (619) 531-2000*

24-hour Emergency Rooms
• *Scripps Hospital, La Jolla: (858) 457-4123*
• *Scripps Mercy Hospital: (619) 294-8111*

Pharmacies
• *CVS: 313 E. Washington • Rite-Aid: 535 Robinson Ave*

Helplines
• *Council of Community Clinics: (619) 542-4300*
• *24-hour Domestic Violence and Sexual Assault Hotline: (888) 385-4657*

Left **Bureau de change** Center **ATM** Right **UPS post boxes**

📑10 Banking & Communications

Exchange
San Diego International Airport has international exchange kiosks in Terminal 1 and Terminal 2. Major banks handle most transactions; bring plenty of ID. Large hotels exchange currency as well, but offer low rates. Exchange windows in San Ysidro handle transactions in dollars and pesos.

ATMs
There are 24-hour Automatic Teller Machines all over the city. Look behind your ATM or credit card to see which banking network it's associated with. ATMs inside convenience stores or malls charge you for the convenience, as does your own bank if you go outside the network.

Banks
Most major banks are found throughout San Diego. Banking hours are usually 9 or 10am–6pm, Monday through Friday, with Saturday hours from 9am–1 or 2pm.

Traveler's Checks
Traveler's checks are good for backup in case your ATM card is swallowed. Most hotels, restaurants, and shops cash them with ID; sometimes banks charge a fee. Checks should always be in US dollars. Personal checks are difficult to cash.

Telephone
If using a telephone at a hotel, ask what the specific charges are first. Coin-operated pay phones can be found at hotels, some restaurants, and at gas stations, but not all of them accept incoming calls. If calling Mexico, dial 011–52 followed by the three-digit city code and seven-digit local number.

Phone Cards
Available all over the city, pre-paid phone cards eliminate the need for coins at public phones. Read the card before buying it; many of them charge a three-minute minimum even if you talk for less than that.

Internet
The San Diego Public Library offers Internet access, as do most hotels. There are many free Wi-Fi spots in restaurants, cafés, and bookstores – the San Diego free Wi-Fi City Guide gives specific information on free Wi-Fi zones across the city.

Post Offices
Regular post office hours are 8:30am–5pm Mon–Fri, with some branches open on Saturday mornings. Stamps are usually available from vending machines in the lobby, and signage indicates the cost of postage for mail sent to domestic and international addresses. Hotel concierges can post mail for you.

Shipping
Franchised United Parcel Service stores throughout the city will package and ship for you. Regular parcel post at the post office is the cheapest, and some branches sell boxes and tape. Packages shipped internationally can take over a month for delivery.

Courier Services
Federal Express and UPS have guaranteed overnight delivery and reliable international service, as does DHL. Many offices sell packaging supplies. Much cheaper, the US Postal Service offers overnight service in the continental US and two–three day service internationally.

Directory

Exchange
• Travelex: 177 Westfield Horton Plaza

Internet
• San Diego free Wi-Fi City Guide: www.openwifispots.com

Post Offices
• Downtown: 815 E. St

Courier Services
• DHL: (800) 225-5345
• FedEx: (800) 463-3339
• UPS: (800) 742-5877

It's rare to find computer terminals anywhere, so you will need a laptop or smart phone to access free Wi-Fi across the city.

Left **Pilar's Beachwear shop at Mission Bay Beach** Right **Drugstore in Tijuana**

⁧10⁩ Shopping Tips

1 Bargaining in Mexico

Bargaining is an ancient art and social exchange in Mexico. The rule of thumb is to offer half the asking price and work up from there. If the vendor senses you really want an item, he or she will stand firm. Remain polite and remember the vendor needs to earn a living. Department stores, upscale shops, and restaurants all have fixed prices.

2 Kobey's Swap Meet

Wear comfortable shoes, bring cash, and come early to walk the 21 aisles of this enormous outdoor flea market. Merchants sell clothing, plants, jewelry, luggage, electronics, sporting goods, and much more. Always ask sellers: "Is that your best price?"

3 Shopping Malls

The best shopping mall bargains can be found around public holidays. Department stores sometimes bring in outside merchandise to sell at "bargain" prices. Malls with concierge services sometimes have discount booklets.

4 Outlet Centers

San Diego has three major outlet centers within an hour's driving distance: the Carlsbad Premium Outlets in North County, the Las Americas Premium Outlets at San Ysidro, and Viejas Outlet Center on the Viejas Indian Reservation east on I-8. You can usually find good deals at the designer spin-off shops.

5 Garage Sales

To meet San Diegans, drive around residential areas on any given Saturday and you'll find them selling items in their driveways. To locate garage sales, look for signs posted on telephone poles or find a copy of the *Pennysaver*, which lists addresses.

6 Senior Discounts

Senior discounts are offered at movie halls, restaurants, hotels, and shops. Some theater chains deem senior status at age 55, and many retail stores designate a certain day of the week for senior discounts. Use your AARP (American Association of Retired Persons) card when booking hotels.

7 Taxes

Current sales tax in San Diego County is 7.75 percent, though city taxes can add another 0.5–1 percent, depending on the location. A non-refundable sales tax is added to all retail purchases and restaurant checks. Food items in grocery stores are not taxed unless they are for immediate consumption. If a store is shipping your purchase to an out-of-state address, you shouldn't pay sales tax. Hotel tax is 10.5 percent.

8 Shopping Hours

Retail shops usually open at 10am and close at 5 or 6pm. Regular hours at shopping malls are 10am–9pm Mon–Sat and 11am–7pm Sun. Department stores sometimes open at 7am for super sales or extend their hours during the Christmas season. Malls close only during a few major holidays.

9 Open 24 Hours

You shouldn't have any trouble finding a 24-hour convenience store selling groceries. Many Ralph's and Albertson's supermarkets are open all night. A 24-hour CVS *(see p110)* has grocery items, and some office supplies can be found at FedEx Office.

10 Returns

Most stores accept returns, unless the item was bought on sale. Stores usually post their returns policy in a prominent place. Many accept returns for in-store credit only.

Left **Farmers' market** Right **Liquor bottles for sale in Tijuana**

🔟 Eating & Accommodation Tips

1 Farmers' Markets
Local farmers sell fresh vegetables, fruit, and specialties such as tamales, cheese and bread at special markets around the city. Seasonal produce is usually of much better quality and price than at the supermarket. Take a supply of single dollar bills to make quick purchases.

2 Lunches & Early Bird Dinners
Entrées on the lunch menu are often less than half the price of those at dinner. Some restaurants offer early-bird dinners from 4–6pm, with a limited number of entrées at a considerable discount.

3 Picnics
Make the most of San Diego's beautiful parks and beaches. Get items to go from restaurants, or stop by markets such as Trader Joe's (see p99) in Pacific Beach to pick up salads, sushi, and deli items.

4 Tipping
Most food servers expect a 15–20 percent tip; leave it in cash or add it to your credit card bill. If the service is truly awful, you're not obliged to tip. With large parties, 18 percent gratuity may be automatically added to the check.

5 Alcohol Age Limit
The legal drinking age in California is 21.

If you look under 30, restaurant servers and merchants selling alcohol will ask to see your photo identification. In Tijuana, the legal drinking age is 18.

6 Fast Food
Fast food restaurants are the cheapest way to eat, are easily found, and many are open all night. San Diego is the birthplace to two fast food chains, Rubio's and Jack-in-the-Box.

7 Happy Hours
Many restaurants and bars offer happy hours on weekdays. For the price of a drink and a few dollars, snack on anything from a hot buffet to chips and dip. Some Mexican restaurants sell cheap tacos on "Taco Tuesdays." Check out the advertisements in the San Diego Reader (see p104).

8 Motel Chains
Staying at a motel chain offers standardized accommodation. Most major chains can be found in Mission Valley's Hotel Circle. Parking is generally free, breakfast is often supplied, and you aren't charged countless petty fees.

9 Apartments & Extended Stay
If you plan to stay in San Diego for more than a few weeks, consider renting an apartment.

Summer rentals, especially along the beach, are more costly. Always ask what amenities are included.

10 Camping
The only comfortable place to camp legally near the city is in Chula Vista. The well-located campground offers a swimming pool, hot tub, and bicycle rentals. If desperate, try sleeping at the airport, or rent a cheap car and sleep in a motel parking lot. RV owners can try Campland on the Bay, who also accept tent campers.

Directory

Farmers' Markets
• 3960 Normal St, Hillcrest: 9am–1pm Sun
• 1st & B, Coronado: 2:30–6pm Tue
• Ocean Beach: 4–8pm Wed
• Horton Square: 225 Broadway 11am–3pm Thu
• Mission Blvd (btw Reed & Pacific Beach Blvd): 8am–noon Sat

Apartment Rentals
• Penny Realty: (866) 522-4116
• San Diego Vacation Rentals: (888) 263-3602

Camping
• San Diego Metro KOA: 111 N. 2nd Ave, Chula Vista, (619) 427-3601
• Campland On the Bay: 2211 Pacific Beach Dr, (858) 581-4200

Left **The Lodge at Torrey Pines** Right **Façade of W**

🔟 Luxury Hotels

1 The Lodge at Torrey Pines
Located on the cliffs of Torrey Pines, this lodge offers exquisite accommodation. Rooms look out onto a courtyard which reflects the surrounding coastal environment and the greens of the Torrey Pines Golf Course. Early California Impressionist art graces the walls and signature restaurant. 🕭 *Map D2 • 11480 N. Torrey Pines Rd, La Jolla • (858) 453-4420 • www.lodgetorreypines. com • $$$$$*

2 Hilton San Diego Gaslamp Quarter
Beautifully appointed rooms with down comforters, loft apartments, and individual attention from the staff make this downtown's best choice. It's located right next to the Convention Center, the Gaslamp Quarter, and Petco Park. 🕭 *Map K6 • 401 K St • (619) 231-4040 • www.hilton.com • $$$$$*

3 Westgate
No expense was spared in re-creating the anteroom of the Palace of Versailles in the front lobby. Baccarat crystal chandeliers, Persian carpets, and French tapestries are just backdrops to the gracious service. European furniture graces rooms equipped with marble baths. 🕭 *Map J4 • 1055 2nd Ave • (619) 238-1818 • www.westgatehotel. com • $$$$$*

4 W
Everyone wants to be part of the W's hip weekend scene. It's all about sleek design and "anytime, anywhere" service. The rooms are fun and have window seats. 🕭 *Map H4 • 421 West B St • (619) 398-3100 • www. starwoodhotels.com • $$$$$*

5 Hotel Parisi
The Mediterranean meets Feng Shui design in this boutique hotel. The rooms are tranquil and minimalist, yet hip. Try one of the 30 in-room spa treatments and then roll into Egyptian cotton sheets and a goose down duvet. 🕭 *Map N2 • 1111 Prospect St, La Jolla • (858) 454-1511 • www. hotelparisi.com • $$$$$*

6 Coronado Island Marriott Resort and Spa
Lush grounds with a few flamingos, a relaxed ambience, and a dedicated staff make this resort a top choice. A California and French styling decorates large, comfy rooms, with the best ones looking out across the bay to San Diego. The hotel runs a water taxi service. 🕭 *Map C6 • 2000 2nd St, Coronado • (619) 435-3000 • www.marriott. com/sanci • $$$$*

7 Pacific Terrace
Sunset views over the Pacific define high living at one of San Diego's finest beach hotels. Large guest rooms come with a balcony or patio. There's no full-service restaurant, but the friendly staff can suggest neighborhood choices. 🕭 *Map A3 • 610 Diamond St • (858) 581-3500 • www. pacificterrace.com • $$$$*

8 Hotel Solamar
This hip boutique hotel in the Gaslamp Quarter offers a complimentary wine hour every evening in the fireplace lounge. California cuisine features at the JSix restaurant, and the fourth-floor pool deck with J6Bar and fire pits is popular with locals and visitors. 🕭 *Map J5 • 435 6th Ave • (619) 819-9500 • www. hotelsolamar.com • $$$$$*

9 Manchester Grand Hyatt San Diego
Two high-rise towers hold 1,625 rooms, many with personal work areas and all with high-speed Internet. The lounge on the 40th floor is one of San Diego's best. 🕭 *Map H5 • 1 Market Place • (619) 232-1234 • www.manchester grand.hyatt.com • $$$$$*

10 Hotel Indigo
Rooms at this trendy boutique hotel in the Gaslamp Quarter come with plush bedding, hardwood floors, and complimentary Internet access. The bar terrace overlooks Petco Park. 🕭 *Map J5 • 509 9th Ave • (619) 727-4000 • www. hotelindigo.com • $$$*

Unless otherwise stated, all hotels accept credit cards, have private bathrooms, air conditioning, and provide dis. access.

La Valencia

Price Categories

For a standard double room per night (with breakfast if included), taxes and extra charges.	**$** under $100
	$$ $100–200
	$$$ $200–250
	$$$$ $250–300
	$$$$$ over $300

🏅 Heritage & Vintage Hotels

1 Hotel del Coronado
This National Historic Landmark re-creates a bygone golden age. Suites in the original Victorian building have balconies that face a lovely white-sand beach. Restaurants, boutiques, and swimming pools add to the aristocratic character. ✪ Map C6
• 1500 Orange Ave, Coronado • (619) 435-6611 • www.hoteldel.com • $$$$$

2 La Valencia
Since 1926, the "Pink Lady of La Jolla" has enchanted with its splendid Mediterranean ambience, exquisite decor, and ideal location on the cliffs above La Jolla Cove. Rooms vary from quite small to large ocean villas. ✪ Map N2
• 1132 Prospect St, La Jolla • (858) 454-0771 • www.lavalencia.com • $$$$$

3 Horton Grand Hotel
Rebuilt from two Victorian-era hotels, this hotel reflects the character of the Gaslamp Quarter. Rooms are individually decorated in period style and each has a gas fireplace.
✪ Map J5 • 311 Island Ave • (619) 544-1886 • www.hortongrand.com • $$$

4 U.S. Grant
Ulysses S. Grant Jr. commissioned this stately 1910 Renaissance palace. A $56-million renovation has restored its past glory, with mahogany furniture and paneling, tile floors, and luxurious rooms. ✪ Map J4 • 326 Broadway • (619) 232-3121 • www.usgrant.net • $$$$$

5 Gaslamp Plaza Suites
Now on the National Register of Historic Places, much of the 1913 craftsmanship of this building remains, such as Australian gumwood, Corinthian marble, and an elevator door made of brass. Complimentary breakfast is served on the rooftop terrace.
✪ Map K4 • 520 E St • (619) 232-9500 • www.gaslampplaza.com • $$$

6 Glorietta Bay Inn
Many of the original fixtures of John D. Spreckels' (see p25) 1908 Edwardian mansion remain, including handmade plaster moldings, chandeliers, and a marble staircase. Splurge on one of the antique-filled guest rooms inside the house. ✪ Map C6 • 1630 Glorietta Blvd, Coronado • (619) 435-3101 • www.gloriettabayinn.com • $$$$

7 The Grande Colonial
La Jolla's first hotel was designed by Richard Requa. The 1913 building houses luxury suites, while a 1926 building contains the main hotel. Elegantly appointed rooms are in keeping with the hotel's European ambience. ✪ Map N3
• 910 Prospect St, La Jolla • (888) 828-5498 • www.thegrandecolonial.com • $$$$

8 Balboa Park Inn
This B&B is housed in Spanish-Colonial style buildings constructed in 1915. The Orient Express room features a Chinese rosewood bed, and the Beach House is decorated in shades of ocean blue. ✪ Map D5 • 3402 Park Blvd • (619) 298-0823 • No dis. access • www.balboaparkinn.com • $$

9 Inn at the Park
This 1926 inn was popular with Hollywood celebrities en route to holidays in Mexico in the 1920s and 30s. The original fixtures lend a delightful retro touch.
✪ Map C5 • 525 Spruce St • (619) 291-0999 • No air conditioning • No dis. access • www.shellhospitality.com • $$

10 The Inn at Rancho Santa Fe
Refined elegance distinguishes this romantic country inn. Many of the red-roofed adobe casitas scattered about the lush grounds boast comfy queen-sized beds, fireplaces, and kitchens. ✪ Map E2 • 5951 Linea del Cielo, Rancho Santa Fe • (858) 756-1131 • www.theinnatrsf.com • $$$$

Left **Façade of San Diego Marriott Hotel & Marina** Right **Fountain at Westin Gaslamp Quarter**

Business Hotels

1 San Diego Marriott Hotel & Marina

Most rooms at this busy hotel are set up with worktables and high-speed Internet. The marina and waterfall swimming pool make great distractions. ◎ Map J6 • 333 W. Harbor Dr • (619) 234-1500 • www. marriotthotels.com • $$$$

2 Omni San Diego Hotel

A skyway links the hotel to Petco Park, and you can even see the ball field from some rooms. Comfy rooms sport great bathrooms, and if you must tend to business, the Convention Center is a few blocks away. ◎ Map K6 • 675 L St • (619) 231-6664 • www. omnihotels.com • $$$$

3 Westin San Diego Hotel

You can't miss this hotel's green silhouette of hexagonal glass towers. Amenities include ergonomic work chairs and high-speed Internet access. The Convention Center is within walking distance. ◎ Map H4 • 400 W. Broadway • (619) 239-4500 • www.westinsandiego. com • $$$

4 Westin Gaslamp Quarter San Diego

Attached to Westfield Horton Plaza, this downtown hotel is close to restaurants and

entertainment venues. Business travelers appreciate the workout room and swimming pool. Gaslamp and the Convention Center are within walking distance. ◎ Map J4 • 910 Broadway Cir • (619) 239-2200 • www. starwoodhotels.com • $$$$

5 Embassy Suites Hotel San Diego Bay – Downtown

Guests enjoy spacious suites that have a living area and a separate bedroom. All rooms open onto a palm tree-filled atrium and a view of the bay or city. Ask for the complimentary airport transportation. ◎ Map H5 • 601 Pacific Hwy • (619) 239-2400 • www.embassy suites.com • $$$

6 Sheraton San Diego Hotel & Marina

Conveniently located near the aiport, this immense property has over 1,000 rooms, bike paths, a marina, a tennis court, and a swimming pool. ◎ Map C5 • 1380 Harbor Island Dr • (619) 291-2900 • www. starwoodhotels.com • $$

7 Hilton La Jolla Torrey Pines

This low key but chic hotel is located next to the Torrey Pines Golf Course. A valet can look after your immediate needs, and a car service is available to drive you to La Jolla. All

rooms have balconies or terraces and many have ocean or harbor views. ◎ Map D2 • 10950 N. Torrey Pines Rd, La Jolla • (858) 558-1500 • www. hilton.com • $$$$$

8 San Diego Marriott Mission Valley

At this hotel, a business center and accommodating staff attract a regular business clientele. Take advantage of the swimming pool, fitness room, tennis courts, and jogging trail. ◎ Map D4 • 8757 Rio San Diego Dr • (619) 692-3800 • www. marriotthotels.com • $$

9 Town & Country Resort & Convention Center

This sprawling family-owned resort has an onsite convention center and 1,000 rooms. Next door is a golf course, a trolley stop, and the Fashion Valley Mall. ◎ Map C4 • 500 Hotel Circle N • (619) 291-7131 • www. towncountry.com • $$

10 Hyatt Regency La Jolla

Post-Modern architect Michael Graves designed this Italian-style palace hotel. A large fitness spa and highly acclaimed restaurants are next door. Business travelers appreciate the business center. ◎ Map B1 • 3777 La Jolla Village Dr, La Jolla • (858) 552-1234 • www. lajollahyatt.com • $$$

Unless otherwise stated, all hotels accept credit cards, have private bathrooms, air conditioning, and provide dis. access.

Best Western Hacienda Hotel Old Town

🔟 Moderately Priced Hotels

1 Humphrey's Half Moon Inn & Suites
Its summer concert series *(see p51)*, tropical landscaping, private marina, and long list of activities make this hotel an entertaining choice. Pay a little more to get a room with a view of the bay. ⬥ Map B5 • 2303 Shelter Island Dr • (619) 224-3411 • www.halfmooninn.com • $$

2 El Cordova
At this 1902 Spanish-style hotel, Mexican tiles line stairways and wrought-iron balconies overlook the street. A swimming pool is set amid lush landscaping, and there are good on-site restaurants. ⬥ Map C6 • 1351 Orange Ave, Coronado • (619) 435-0632 • www.elcordovahotel.com • $$$

3 Best Western Hacienda Hotel Old Town
On a hillside overlooking Old Town, the rooms at this charming hacienda-style hotel have private balconies or look onto a courtyard. Free airport transportation. ⬥ Map P5 • 4041 Harney St • (800) 888-1991 • www.bestwestern.com • $$

4 Crowne Plaza San Diego
In the 1960s, a wave of Polynesian-themed hotels sprang up and those that survived have almost a retro coolness factor to them. The tropical decor still rules the public areas, but the rooms are contemporary and overlook the pool or neighboring golf course. ⬥ Map Q4 • 2270 Hotel Circle N • (619) 297-1101 • www.cp-sandiego.com • $$

5 The Dana on Mission Bay
Families love this hotel. All the water activities of Mission Bay are close by, and the hotel operates free shuttles to SeaWorld. Tropical landscaping surrounds the grounds, and the swimming pool is a hit with kids. Free parking. ⬥ Map B4 • 1710 W. Mission Bay Dr • (619) 222-6440 • www.thedana.com • $$

6 The Coronado Village Inn
This European-style B&B offers individually decorated rooms with antiques and lacy comforters. A full kitchen is available to guests, and there is a daily Continental breakfast. ⬥ Map C6 • 1017 Park Place, Coronado • (619) 435-9318 • No air conditioning • www.coronadovillageinn.com • $$

7 Fairfield Inn & Suites San Diego Old Town
Spanish-Colonial architecture befits the neighborhood's origins, and a sunny interior patio provides respite from the streets of Old Town. This above-average Holiday Inn offers a free breakfast buffet and a swimming pool. ⬥ Map P6 • 3900 Old Town Ave • (619) 299-7400 • www.marriott.com • $$

8 Bay Club Hotel & Marina
Rattan furniture and tropical fabrics give a Polynesian cast to this hotel. The best rooms are at the back, and have views of the marina and Point Loma. Breakfast is included. ⬥ Map B5 • 2131 Shelter Island Dr • (619) 224-8888 • www.bayclubhotel.com • $$

9 Inn Sunset Cliffs
A 180-degree ocean view distinguishes this inn. Many rooms have kitchens, and a whirlpool tub in the presidential suite overlooks the sea. A swimming pool is located between rooms. ⬥ Map A5 • 1370 Sunset Cliffs Blvd • (619) 222-7901 • www.innatsunsetcliffs.com • $$$

10 Les Artistes
Rooms are named and decorated after famous artists, such as the tropical Gauguin room, the French-country Monet, and the rustic Mexican look inspired by muralist Diego Rivera. The Japanese-style Furo room has a soaking tub. ⬥ Map D2 • 944 Camino del Mar, Del Mar • (858) 755-4646 • No air conditioning • www.lesartistesinn.com • $$

Hilton San Diego Resort

🔟 Waterfront Hotels

1 Crystal Pier Hotel
Reservations are essential for these 1927 Cape Cod-style cottages which sit directly on the pier. Many have kitchenettes, and patios with views of Pacific Beach. 🚫 Map A3 • 4500 Ocean Blvd • (858) 483-6983 • No dis. access • www.crystalpier.com • $$$$

2 Catamaran Resort Hotel
This Polynesian-themed hotel offers a long list of water activities. Within walking distance to many restaurants, Tiki torches light your way through lushly landscaped grounds. The upper floors of the towers have great views. 🚫 Map A3 • 3999 Mission Blvd • (858) 488-1081 • www.catamaran resort.com • $$$$

3 Hilton San Diego Resort
Mediterranean in style, this resort is perfectly located to watch the evening fireworks at SeaWorld. Kid's Klub can keep the kids entertained as you relax at the enormous swimming pool or spa. The best rooms are near the bay. 🚫 Map B3 • 1775 E Mission Bay Dr • (619) 276-4010 • www.hilton.com • $$$$

4 Harbor Vacations Club
At San Diego's most unique hotel, you have a choice to stay in eight different yachts, from a sailing catamaran to a 55-ft (17-m) coast cruiser. These floating dockside villas have a cooking galley and luxury cabins. 🚫 Map B5 • Marina Cortez, 1880 Harbor Island Dr, G-Dock • (619) 297-9484 • No dis. access • www.shell vacationsclub.com • $$$

5 Bahia Resort Hotel
This venerable Mission Bay Hotel is right next to the bay and Mission Beach. At night, you can enjoy live music on the Bahia Belle, a sternwheeler that floats on the bay every evening. 🚫 Map A4 • 998 W. Mission Bay Dr • (858) 488-0551 • No dis. access • www.bahiahotel.com • $$$

6 The Beach Cottages
Detached cottages with full kitchens and laundry facilities are a good option for families who don't need luxury. Other accommodation choices include apartments and basic, inexpensive motel rooms. 🚫 Map A3 • 4255 Ocean Blvd • (858) 483-7440 • No air conditioning • www.beachcottages.com • $$$$

7 Ocean Park Inn
Restaurants are within walking distance of this contemporary inn, and the boardwalk action is just outside the door. Quiet rooms with the best views are on the third floor. All rooms feature a balcony or patio. 🚫 Map A3 • 710 Grand Ave • (858) 483-5858 • www.oceanparkinn.com • $$$

8 Best Western Blue Sea Lodge
Head to the pool or the Pacific Ocean for a morning swim and then down the boardwalk for breakfast. New rooms and suites have brightened this lodge, but the older rooms have the beach view. 🚫 Map A3 • 707 Pacific Beach Dr • (858) 488-4700 • www.bestwest ern-bluesea.com • $$$

9 Carlsbad Inn Beach Resort
Families love this sprawling resort. Rooms and time-share condominiums are available nightly or weekly. Several activities and classes are held daily, and there's a good Mexican restaurant. 🚫 Map D1 • 3075 Carlsbad Blvd, Carlsbad • (760) 434-7020 • www.carlsbadinn.com • $$$

10 Oceanside Marina Suites
Surrounded by water on three sides, large, breezy rooms have lovely views. Suites are great value with a balcony, kitchen, and fireplace. During summer, a boat ferries guests to a miles-long beach. 🚫 Map D1 • 2008 Harbor Dr. N, Oceanside • (760) 722-1561 • No air conditioning • www.omihotel.com • $$

Unless otherwise stated, all hotels accept credit cards, have private bathrooms, air conditioning, and provide dis. access.

Paradise Point Resort & Spa

Spas

1 Four Seasons Residence Club Aviara
With impeccable service and a superb setting, this property is one of the most highly rated in Southern California. Choose between indoor and outdoor treatment rooms, or a couple's suite with a whirlpool. ◈ *Map D1 • 7210 Blue Heron Place • (760) 603-3700 • www.fourseasons. com/aviara • $$$$$*

2 Golden Door
Modeled after the ancient *honjin* inns, Japanese gardens, streams, and waterfalls make a glorious backdrop to a week of fitness and meditation. For most of the year, the spa is a women-only domain. ◈ *Map E2 • 777 Deer Springs Rd, San Marcos • No dis. access • (760) 744-5777 • www.golden door.com • $$$$$*

3 La Costa Resort & Spa
The Spanish-Colonial complex contains two PGA championship golf courses, a tennis center, a spa with assorted massage and body treatments, and a fitness room. ◈ *Map D1 • 2100 Costa del Mar Rd, Carlsbad • (760) 438-9111 • www. lacosta.com • $$$$$*

4 Loews Coronado Bay Resort
The "Sea Spa" at this self-contained resort includes Watsu, which combines the buoyancy of water and the pressure techniques of Shiatsu massage. For an ultimate splurge, check into one of the bayside villas with views across San Diego Bay. ◈ *Map E2 • 4000 Coronado Bay Rd, Coronado • (619) 424-4000 • www.loewshotels. com • $$$$*

5 Rancho Valencia Resort
Bougainvillea cascades over the Spanish *casitas* in this stunning resort. Many rooms feature cathedral ceilings, private terraces, and fireplaces. Rejuvenation treatments include reflexology, aromatherapy treatments and various massages. ◈ *Map E2 • 5921 Valencia Circle, Rancho Santa Fe • (858) 756-1123 • www. ranchovalencia.com • $$$$$*

6 Cal-a-Vie
Exhilarating programs focus on fitness, nutrition, and personal care. The Mediterranean-style villas provide the most luxurious accommodation. ◈ *Map E1 • 29402 Spa Havens Rd, Vista • (760) 842-6831 • www. calavie.com • $$$$$*

7 L'Auberge Del Mar Resort & Spa
Join the list of Hollywood notables who relax at this boutique hotel and spa near the Pacific. The rooms feature marble baths and many have private balconies and fireplaces. ◈ *Map D2 • 1540 Camino del Mar, Del Mar • (858) 259-1515 • www.lauberge delmar.com • $$$$$*

8 Rancho Bernardo Inn
Two-story, red-tile-roof adobe buildings and bougainvillea-adorned patios evoke images of early California at this gracious resort. Life here revolves around the adjoining golf course, spa or tennis courts. ◈ *Map E2 • 17550 Bernardo Oaks Dr, Rancho Bernardo • (877) 517-9340 • www.rancho bernardoinn.com • $$$*

9 Paradise Point Resort & Spa
At this Indonesian-style spa, jasmine-scented or hot stone massages can precede a soak in a rose petal bedecked tub. The brightly decorated cottage rooms have private lanais. ◈ *Map B4 • 1404 Vacation Rd • (858) 274-4630 • www.paradisepoint. com • $$$$$*

10 Rancho La Puerta
Since 1940, guests have pursued body and mind fitness at this beautiful Mexican-Colonial style resort. Lodgings are in *casitas* decorated with folk art and bright fabrics. The dining room specializes in homegrown organic food. ◈ *Map F3 • 476 Tecate Rd, Tecate, Baja California, Mexico • (858) 764-5500 • www.rancho lapuerta.com • $$$$$*

The Golden Door is considered America's best spa. The Japanese honjin inns were places where travelers could come to rest.

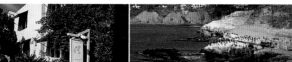

Left **B&B Inn La Jolla** Right **View from B&B Inn La Jolla**

Bed & Breakfasts

Britt Scripps Inn
This luxurious Victorian inn near Balboa Park has nine rooms with antique furniture, lush fabrics, and modern conveniences. Guests enjoy freshly cooked breakfasts each morning and artisan cheeses with wine in the parlor each afternoon. ❧ Map J1 • 406 Maple St • (619) 230-1991 • www.brittscripps.com • $$$$

B&B Inn La Jolla
This delightful home with its individually decorated rooms was designed in 1913 by renowned architect Irving Gill, and Kate Sessions *(see p19)* planted its original gardens. ❧ Map N3 • 7753 Draper Ave, La Jolla • (858) 456-2066 • www.innlajolla.com • $$$

Keating House
The vintage 1888 Queen Anne home and adjoining 1905 cottage have been restored to Victorian perfection. Ask the hosts about the benevolent ghost that haunts the inn. ❧ Map J2 • 2331 2nd Ave • (619) 239-8585 • No dis. access • www.keatinghouse.com • $$

The Cottage
This city hideaway surrounded by a herb garden has two rooms with king-size beds and private entrances. The "Cottage" is furnished with unique Victorian antiques such as a wood burning stove; the "Garden Room" is in the owners' home. ❧ Map C4 • 3829 Albatross St • (619) 299-1564 • No dis. access • No air conditioning • www.cottagevacation.us • $$

Elsbree House
Close to the beach and many restaurants and shops of Ocean Beach is this peaceful, cottage-style B&B. A home-cooked breakfast is served, and the owners are knowledgeable about San Diego. ❧ Map A4 • 5054 Narragansett Ave • (619) 226-4133 • www.bbinnob.com • $$

Crone's Cobblestone Cottage B&B
At this restored 1913 Craftsman-style bungalow, choose either the Elliot or the Eaton room, both furnished with period antiques. The walls are lined with thousands of volumes. ❧ Map C4 • 1302 Washington Place • (619) 295-4765 • No credit cards • Shared bath • No air conditioning • www.cronescobblestonebandb.com • $$

Cardiff-by-the-Sea Lodge
Rooms at this romantic seaside hideaway can be either contemporary in design or borderline Victorian. In the Sweetheart Room, find a heart-shaped tub and a sweeping ocean view. Many rooms feature four poster beds, ocean views, and fireplaces. ❧ Map D2 • 142 Chesterfield Dr, Cardiff-by-the-Sea • (760) 944-6474 • www.cardifflodge.com • $$

The Inn at Europa Village
Ideally situated for touring the Temecula vineyards, rooms in this Mission-style inn have private balconies, Jacuzzis, and fireplaces. Rates include a continental breakfast with fresh pastries. ❧ Map E1 • 33350 La Serena Way, Temecula • (951) 676-7047 • www.europavillage.com • $$

Orchard Hill Country Inn
At this most luxurious of Julian's B&B inns, pick a Craftsman-style cottage with a whirlpool tub, fireplace, and private porch. Tasty breakfasts make a good start to the day. ❧ Map F2 • 2502 Washington St, Julian • (760) 765-1700 • www.orchardhill.com • $$$

Julian Gold Rush Hotel
Built in 1897 by a freed slave from Missouri, this quaint inn is the oldest continually operating hotel in Southern California. Its lacy curtains might remind you of your grandma's house. ❧ Map F2 • 2032 Main St, Julian • (760) 765-0201 • No dis. access • No air conditioning • www.julianhotel.com • $$

Unless otherwise stated, all hotels accept credit cards, have private bathrooms, air conditioning, and provide dis. access.

USA Hostels Gaslamp

Price Categories

For a standard double room per night (with breakfast if included), taxes and extra charges.	**$** under $100
	$$ $100–200
	$$$ $200–250
	$$$$ $250–300
	$$$$$ over $300

🔟 Budget Hotels & Hostels

1 La Pensione

In the heart of Little Italy, rooms contain a queen bed, TV, and refrigerator. A coin-operated laundry is on the premises, as well as free parking. Great Italian restaurants are just outside. ⌾ Map H3 • 606 W. Date St • (619) 236-8000 • No air conditioning • www.la pensionehotel.com • $$

2 Kings Inn, Hotel Circle

This vintage-styled inn with a swimming pool and spa tub has clean, comfortable rooms and friendly, helpful staff. Good onsite restaurants serve breakfast, lunch, and dinner. ⌾ Map C4 • 1333 Hotel Circle S. • (619) 297-2231 • www. kingsinnsandiego.com • $$

3 Old Town Inn

Rooms are clean and comfy, and the hotel offers one of the better breakfasts around. An efficiency unit comes with a microwave, refrigerator, and range top. Parking is free. ⌾ Map B4 • 4444 Pacific Hwy • (619) 260-8024 • www.oldtown-inn.com • $

4 Vagabond Inn Point Loma

This motel is well situated for sportfishing activities and the Cabrillo National Monument. Along with the clean and cheery rooms, enjoy the free breakfast, airport shuttle, parking, and the swimming pool. ⌾ Map B5 • 1325 Scott St • (619) 224-3371 • www. vagabondinn.com • $$

5 Days Inn Harbor View

Clean and functional, every room comes with a mini-refrigerator and satellite TV. Amenities include a swimming pool, coin-operated laundry, and a free airport shuttle. The trolley runs to the Convention Center. ⌾ Map H3 • 1919 Pacific Hwy • (619) 232-1077 • www.daysinn.com • $

6 Comfort Inn Gaslamp

Located in the Gaslamp Quarter, close to the Convention Center and Petco Park, is this affordable chain hotel with 100 rooms. Guestrooms have a mini-fridge, a microwave, and free Wi-Fi. A complimentary breakfast is served. ⌾ Map J4 • 660 G. St • (619) 238-4100 • www.comfortinn gaslamp.com • $$

7 Moonlight Beach Motel

This motel is located near shops, restaurants, and Moonlight Beach, one of the county's most highly rated beaches. All rooms have kitchenettes and the third-floor rooms offer great views. ⌾ Map D2 • 233 2nd St, Encinitas • (760) 753-0623 • No air conditioning • www.moon lightbeachmotel.com • $$

8 Ocean Beach International Hostel

Passports and/or air tickets are required for check in. Teachers and out-of-county residents who hold hostel membership cards may also stay. They offer free breakfast and barbecue evenings, a kitchen, videos, and free lockers and airport transport. ⌾ Map A4 • 4961 Newport Ave • (619) 223-7873 • No dis. access • No air conditioning • No private bathrooms • www.california hostel.com • $

9 USA Hostels Gaslamp

Centrally located, they offer dorm and some private rooms, Internet access, a laundry, kitchen, lounge area with videos, free lockers, and all-you-can-make pancake breakfasts. ⌾ Map K5 • 726 5th Ave • (619) 232-3100 • No dis. access • No air conditioning • No private bathrooms • www.usahostels.com • $

10 HI San Diego Downtown Hostel

This bright hostel offers dorm and some private rooms, free airport transport and breakfast, kitchen and lounge facilities, laundry and Internet access. ⌾ Map K5 • 521 Market St • (619) 525-1531 • No dis. access • No air conditioning • No private bathrooms • www. sandiegohostels.org • $

General Index

*Page numbers in **bold** type refer to main entries.*

Acknowledgments

The Author

Born in San Diego, Pamela Barrus is an unapologetic vagabond, having traveled solo through some 200 countries. She is the author of *Dream Sleeps: Castle and Palace Hotels of Europe* and has contributed to a number of national magazines. She still finds San Diego one of the best places in the world to come home to and enjoy the sunshine.

The author would like to thank Mary Barrus and Roger Devenyns for sharing their exceptional knowledge and insight of San Diego with her.

Photographer Chris Stowers

Additional Photography

Max Alexander, Geoff Dann, Frank Greenaway, Derek Hall, Neil Mersh, Rob Reichenfeld, Neil Setchfield, Scott Suchman

Factcheckers Paul Franklin, Nancy Mikula, Paul Skinner

AT DK INDIA:
Managing Editor Aruna Ghose
Art Editor Benu Joshi
Project Editors Anees Saigal, Vandana Bhagra
Editorial Assistance Pamposh Raina
Project Designer Bonita Vaz
Senior Cartographer Uma Bhattacharya
Cartographer Suresh Kumar
Picture Researcher Taiyaba Khatoon
Indexer & Proofreader Bhavna Seth Ranjan
DTP Co-ordinator Shailesh Sharma
DTP Designer Vinod Harish

AT DK LONDON:
Publisher Douglas Amrine
Publishing Manager Lucinda Cooke
Senior Art Editor Marisa Renzullo
Senior Cartographic Editor Casper Morris
Senior DTP Designer Jason Little
DK Picture Library Richard Dabb, Romaine Werblow, Hayley Smith, Gemma Woodward
Production Rita Sinha
Revisions Team Marta Bescos Sanchez, Sonal Bhatt, Louise Cleghorn, Dipika Dasgupta, Neha Dhingra, Nicola Erdpresser, Anna Freiberger, Camilla Gersh, Claire Jones, Juliet Kenny, Maite Lantaron, Jude Ledger, Carly Madden, Carolyn Patten, Rada Radojicic, Meredith Smith, Ajay Verma, Nikhil Verma, Hugo Wilkinson, Ros Walford

Picture Credits

a – above; b – below/bottom; c – centre; l – left; r – right; t – top.

The publishers would like to thank the following for their assistance and kind permission to photograph at their establishments:

Balboa Park, San Diego; San Diego Aerospace Museum; San Diego Automotive Museum; Birch Aquarium; San Diego Chinese Historical Museum; Horton Plaza; San Diego Maritime Museum; San Diego Museum of Art; Santa Fe Depot; Spanish Village Art Center; The Putnam Foundation, Timken Museum of Art, San Diego; Villa Montezuma; San Diego Union Historical Museum; Wells Fargo Museum; and all other churches, missions, museums, parks, hotels, restaurants, and sights too numerous to thank individually. Works of art have been reproduced with the permission of the following copyright holders: The Putnam Foundation, Timken Museum of Art, San Diego: Frans Hals *Portrait of a Gentleman* (1634) 18bc; Alan Bowness, Hepworth Estate, *Figure for Landscape*, Bronze (1960) 18tl.

The publishers would like to thank the following individuals, companies and picture libraries for their kind permission to reproduce their photographs.

ALAMY: MARK Gibson 66tl; Popperfoto 51tr; Robert Harding World Imagery 20-21; Andrew Slayman 22-23c, ZUMA 99tr. BALBOA PARK: Brett Shoaf 66tr; BAZAAR DEL MUNDO: Ted Walton 82tr; BUBBLES BOUTIQUE: 74tl. CORBIS: 14-15c, 38tr, 39tr; Art on File 48t; Bettman 35tl; Jan Butchofsky-Houser 36-37; Anthony Cooper, Ecoscene 107tl; Richard Cummins 10-11c, 25cra, 38tl, 66c, 67tl, 67tr; Raymond Gehman 87bl; Mark E. Gibson 98tr; Philip Gould 52 tl; Kelly Harriger 63tr; Dave G. Houser 1c;

The Mariners Museum 13br; Museum of History & Industry 38c; Fred Greaves/Reuters 12t, 12bl; Bill Ross 24-25c, 88-89; Bob Rowan 62t; G.E. Kidder Smith 38tc; Underwood & Underwood 39bl. HILTON SAN DIEGO RESORT: 118. LA JOLA PLAYHOUSE: 33bc, 50bc; LA VALENCIA: 115tl; THE LODGE AT TORREY PINES: 114tl; LONELY PLANET IMAGES: Richard Cummins 26-27c, 68-69, Anthony Pidgeon 102-103 LUCY 99tl. MASTERFILE: Dale Sanders 4-5 MURPHY O'BRIEN PUBLIC RELATIONS: 56tl. SAN DIEGO HISTORICAL SOCIETY: Tom Ladwig 73bl; SAN DIEGO MUSEUM OF MAN: 75T; SAN DIEGO ZOO & WILD ANIMAL PARK: 2tr, 14tr, 15b, 16tr, 16tl, 16cra, 16bl, 17cr, 52cl, 62cra, 70cl, 94tr. SCRIPPS INSTITUTION OF OCEANOGRAPHY: 33cb. SEAWORLD: 7cr, 30-31c, 30tl, 30crb, 30bc, 31tl, 31cr, 31b, 94cr, 95tr. THORNTON WINERY: 96c.

All other images are © Dorling Kindersley. For further information see www.dkimages.com

Special Editions of DK Travel Guides

DK Travel Guides can be purchased in bulk quantities at discounted prices for use in promotions or as premiums. We are also able to offer special editions and personalized jackets, corporate imprints, and excerpts from all of our books, tailored specifically to meet your own needs.

To find out more, please contact:

(in the US) **SpecialSales@dk.com**

(in the UK) **travelspecialsales@uk.dk.com**

(in Canada) DK Special Sales at **general@tourmaline.ca**

(in Australia) **business.development @pearson.com.au**

Selected Street Index